# Frameworks for Assessing Learning and Development Outcomes

Terrell L. Strayhorn
*Principal Author*

Don G. Creamer
Ted K. Miller
Jan Arminio
*Consulting Editors*

In consultation with an advisory committee consisting
of representatives from CAS member organizations.

2006

Council for the Advancement
of Standards in Higher Education

Frameworks for Assessing Learning and Development Outcomes
© Copyright 2006 by the Council for the Advancement of Standards in Higher Education

**Library of Congress Cataloging-in-Publication Data**
Strayhorn, Terrell L.
Frameworks for Assessing Learning and Development Outcomes
Includes bibliographical references.
Consulting Editors: Don G. Creamer, Ted K. Miller, and Jan Arminio

ISBN 1-58328-039-1
1. Student Affairs, 2. Student Services, 3. Professional Standards,
4. Assessment, 5. Higher Education, 6. Learning Outcomes

**CAS Officers**
President: Jan L. Arminio, NACA, Shippensburg University
Treasurer: Carmen G. Neuberger, Public Director
Secretary: Douglas K. Lange, AFA, Evolve Learning, Inc.
At-Large: Paula L. Swinford, ACHA, University of Southern California
At-Large: Susan R. Komives, ACPA, University of Maryland
At-Large, Publications Editor: Laura A. Dean, ACCA, University of Georgia
CAS Executive Director: Phyllis L. Mable

Interior Design: Laura Dugan, HBP, Hagerstown, MD
Cover Design: Laura Dugan, HBP, Hagerstown, MD
Printing and Binding: HBP, Inc., Hagerstown, MD


Permission is granted to use this document, or portions thereof, to serve the purposes of institutions of higher learning and their student support programs and services to promote program self-assessment and development and professional staff development in pursuit of enhanced educational environments to benefit college student learning and development. This permission is contingent upon appropriate credit being given to the Council for the Advancement of Standards in Higher Education (CAS). Permission must be sought for commercial use of content from this publication, when the material is quoted in advertising, when portions are used in other publications, or when charges for copies are made.


**CAS STANDARDS DISCLAIMER**
The standards and guidelines published in "CAS Professional Standards for Higher Education" by the Council for the Advancement of Standards in Higher Education (CAS) and referred to in each of the "CAS Self-Assessment Guides" (SAGs) are developed through the voluntary efforts of leaders of professional associations in higher education. The purpose of the standards and guidelines is to identify criteria and principles by which institutions may choose to assess and enhance various areas of their academic, administrative, or student affairs programs and services. CAS specifically disclaims any liability or responsibility for any perceived or actual shortcomings inherent in the text or application of the standards. Further, CAS does not certify individuals nor accredit programs. No institution, whether it has met some or all of the CAS standards, is authorized to indicate that it is "approved, endorsed, certified, or otherwise sanctioned by CAS." Institutions that have conducted a self-assessment of one or more functional areas addressed by CAS Standards and Guidelines using the appropriate CAS Self-Assessment Guide (SAG), where that self-assessment provides evidence that an institution meets these standards, are free to make accurate representations to the effect that the designated program or service meets the CAS [insert particular Standard title(s)] Standards.


Uses of materials from Frameworks for Assessing Learning and Development Outcomes other than in the cases described above, should be brought to the attention of CAS, One Dupont Circle, NW, Suite 300, Washington, DC 20036-1188; (202) 862-1400; www.cas.edu; All rights reserved.

Dear Reader,

As President of the Council for the Advancement of Standards in Higher Education, I am excited to offer you this valuable assessment resource. The idea of creating a resource that would guide higher educational professionals in assessing learning outcomes was born several years ago. The exact nature of it required considerable thought and consultation. This publication authored by Dr. Terrell Strayhorn is CAS's foray into creating additional assistance in assessing learning development outcomes (FALDOs).

The FALDOs stem from the CAS Standard that mandates each program and service to "provide evidence of its impact on the achievement of student learning and development outcomes" (CAS, 2006). *The Book of Standards* gives 16 learning outcome domains from which learning can be assessed as well as offers examples of learning indicators. More over, the FALDOs take professionals further in guiding learning assessment outcomes. The FALDOs create a bridge between professional standards and assessing learning.

As you will see, an introduction, theoretical context, relevant variables, assessment examples, available instruments, related websites, references, and recommending reading make up the frameworks. I envision that this as a first edition of the FALDOs, with regular subsequent iterations to follow. This first edition provides solid introductory material to the world of assessing outcomes.

I want to thank Dr. Terrell Strayhorn, who authored the FALDOs, which required delving into a vast and diverse literature base. Due to the technical nature of the healthy behavior learning outcome domain and the expertise required of health professionals beyond the traditional higher education preparation, the reader will note that guest authors wrote the healthy behavior framework. I am grateful for the expertise of Dr. Patricia Fabiano, Dr. Richard Keeling, and Dr. Pam Viele as well.

I am sure you will find the FALDOs an important resource for enhancing learning at your institution. On behalf of students who benefit from your thoughtful work, I thank you.

Sincerely,

Jan Arminio, Ph.D.
CAS President

## About the Author

**Terrell L. Strayhorn** is Assistant Professor of Higher Education at The University of Tennessee-Knoxville. He teaches in the master's College Student Personnel Program and the doctoral Higher Education program. Dr. Strayhorn's research interests include the effect of college on students and the influence of educational policy on college student outcomes such as achievement and persistence. His dissertation research focused on graduate student persistence to degree using a nationally representative sample. He earned a masters degree in Educational Policy from The University of Virginia and received his Ph.D. in Educational Leadership and Policy Studies from Virginia Tech. He has authored or co-authored over a dozen journal articles and reports, two book chapters, and has presented over 25 programs at national conferences.

# About the Consulting Editors

**Don G. Creamer** is Professor Emeritus at Virginia Tech located in Blacksburg, Virginia. He served as Professor and Coordinator of the Higher Education and Student Affairs program for 28 years. In addition, Dr. Creamer is Co-Director of the Educational Policy Institute at Virginia Tech and Past President of the CAS for the Advancement of Standards in Higher Education (CAS). He has authored or co-authored more than 60 journal articles, 31 book and monograph chapters, and 11 books or monographs.

**Theodore (Ted) K. Miller** is Professor Emeritus at The University of Georgia in Athens, Georgia where he served as Professor of Counseling and Human Development Services and Coordinator of the Student Development in Higher Education preparation program for 30 years following 10 years of service at the University of Florida and the University of Buffalo. Dr. Miller served as the founding president of the Council for the Advancement of Standards in Higher Education (CAS) and concluded 25 years of service to the consortium as Publications Editor. In addition, he edited and guided the evolution of *The CAS Book of Professional Standards for Higher Education* from 1986 to 2003.

**Jan L. Arminio** is Professor at Shippensburg University in Shippensburg, Pennsylvania, where she is Chair of the Counseling Department. In addition, Dr. Arminio currently serves at president of the Council for the Advancement of Standards in Higher Education (CAS). She has authored numerous works including articles on supervision and qualitative research.

# Acknowledgements

Any project as ambitious as a book on learning outcomes assessment across 16 learning and development domains creates an enormous debt for its author. First, I would like to thank my family for their support throughout the entirety of this project. Special thanks to my parents, siblings, and precious children, Aliyah Brielle and Tionne Lamont. While family allowed me to start the project, my colleagues, mentors, and friends ensured that I completed it. Special thanks to Belinda Bennett and Dr. Susan Komives for their insights on leadership development, Dr. Catherine Amelink for her assistance, and several other graduate students who offered words of encouragement throughout this assignment including Melanie Hayden, Barb Holcomb, Anne Laughlin, Tonya Saddler, and Mario Williams. Many faculty and staff members at Virginia Tech warrant my appreciation for their support during the course of this work. Drs. Joan Hirt, Steve Janosik, and Elizabeth Creamer deserve special mention for allowing this project to take priority when necessary and for supporting the author and editors at conferences and meetings prior to completion of this text. Vicki Meadows lent a helping hand to our team as we were preparing for conferences too. Thanks, Vicki.

Perhaps no one deserves more special recognition for their steadfast contribution to this effort than Dr. Don Creamer and Dr. Ted Miller, the consulting editors. Don's knowledge about assessment and quality in higher education and student affairs helped bring together the foundation of this project. Not only that, but as my dissertation advisor, Don's confidence in my ability to juggle both the dissertation and this book project simultaneously often served as fuel to "burn the midnight oil" and "the early morning candle" at both ends. Ted's careful eye for details and his expertise in scholarly writing brought a wealth of much-needed constructive criticism to each and every document. I owe them both my sincere gratitude.

Finally, the Council for the Advancement of Standards in Higher Education (CAS), the author, and the editors would like to thank the following reviewers for their many helpful comments and suggestions: Jan Arminio, Dorothy Mitstifer, Sam Ratcliffe, Michelle Stefanisko, Paula Swinford, Matthew Weismantel, Susan Komives, and Eric White. For their invaluable assistance, I am indebted to Adrienne Hamcke Wicker and Laura Dean for their incisive copyediting and advice. In addition, we would like to thank all members of the CAS Advisory Committee for this book project.

Terrell L. Strayhorn, Ph.D.
*The University of Tennessee*

# Table of Contents

**Preface** ............................................................................... 1

**Chapter One** ........................................................................ 11

Introduction ........................................................................... 11

Theoretical Context .................................................................. 12

Relevant Variables and Indicators ................................................ 13

Assessment Examples ............................................................... 13

Assessment, Evaluation, and Research Tools ................................. 14

Related Websites ..................................................................... 15

References ............................................................................. 15

Conclusion ............................................................................. 16

**Chapter Two** ........................................................................ 19

Introduction to Assessment ....................................................... 19

General Assessment Considerations ............................................ 19

Technical Issues of Assessment .................................................. 22

Methodological Challenges in Assessment and Research ................ 24

Conclusion ............................................................................. 26

References ............................................................................. 27

FALDO: Career Choices . . . . . . . . . . . . . . . . . . . . . . . . . . . . . . . . . . . . . . . . . . . . . . . . . . . 29

FALDO: Collaboration. . . . . . . . . . . . . . . . . . . . . . . . . . . . . . . . . . . . . . . . . . . . . . . . . . 37

FALDO: Effective Communication . . . . . . . . . . . . . . . . . . . . . . . . . . . . . . . . . . . . . . . . 45

FALDO: Appreciating Diversity . . . . . . . . . . . . . . . . . . . . . . . . . . . . . . . . . . . . . . . . . . 51

FALDO: Personal and Educational Goals . . . . . . . . . . . . . . . . . . . . . . . . . . . . . . . . . . 61

FALDO: Healthy Behavior. . . . . . . . . . . . . . . . . . . . . . . . . . . . . . . . . . . . . . . . . . . . . . . 69

FALDO: Independence. . . . . . . . . . . . . . . . . . . . . . . . . . . . . . . . . . . . . . . . . . . . . . . . . 79

FALDO: Intellectual Growth . . . . . . . . . . . . . . . . . . . . . . . . . . . . . . . . . . . . . . . . . . . . . 87

FALDO: Leadership Development . . . . . . . . . . . . . . . . . . . . . . . . . . . . . . . . . . . . . . . . 93

FALDO: Satisfying and Productive Lifestyles . . . . . . . . . . . . . . . . . . . . . . . . . . . . . . . 101

FALDO: Meaningful Interpersonal Relationships. . . . . . . . . . . . . . . . . . . . . . . . . . . . . 107

FALDO: Realistic Self-Appraisal . . . . . . . . . . . . . . . . . . . . . . . . . . . . . . . . . . . . . . . . . 113

FALDO: Enhanced Self-Esteem. . . . . . . . . . . . . . . . . . . . . . . . . . . . . . . . . . . . . . . . . . 119

FALDO: Social Responsibility . . . . . . . . . . . . . . . . . . . . . . . . . . . . . . . . . . . . . . . . . . . 127

FALDO: Spiritual Awareness. . . . . . . . . . . . . . . . . . . . . . . . . . . . . . . . . . . . . . . . . . . . 135

FALDO: Clarified Values. . . . . . . . . . . . . . . . . . . . . . . . . . . . . . . . . . . . . . . . . . . . . . . 141

Epilogue. . . . . . . . . . . . . . . . . . . . . . . . . . . . . . . . . . . . . . . . . . . . . . . . . . . . . . . . . . . 147

References . . . . . . . . . . . . . . . . . . . . . . . . . . . . . . . . . . . . . . . . . . . . . . . . . . . . . . . . 153

# Preface

The Council for the Advancement of Standards in Higher Education (CAS) was established over a quarter century ago for purposes of developing and promulgating standards of professional practice to guide higher education practitioners and their institutions, especially in regard to work with college students. Currently, the CAS Board of Directors is composed of delegates from 36 professional higher education associations in the United States and Canada. These organizations represent a full-range of not-for-profit corporations concerned with student learning and development, many of which identify with the field of student affairs. In addition to the functional area practice standards, CAS has adopted and promulgated a set of master's level academic program standards to guide the graduate education of student affairs entry-level administrators. (Miller, 2003, p. 1)

The standards and guidelines for over 30 functional areas along with a description of their historical evolutions and contextual settings are included in *The Book of Professional Standards for Higher Education*. Also included are the General Standards that are consistent in all the sets of standards CAS publishes. These serve as a foundation upon which more specific Standards and Guidelines are added. The General Standards are offered below.

## CAS General Standards and Guidelines 2003

*Part 1: Mission*

**Each program and service in higher education must incorporate student learning and student development in its mission. The program and service must enhance overall educational experiences. The program and service must develop, record, disseminate, implement, and regularly review its mission and goals. Mission statements must be consistent with the mission and goals of the institution and with the standards in this document. The program and service must operate as an integral part of the institution's overall mission.**

*Part 2: Program*

**The formal education of students consists of the curriculum and the co-curriculum, and must promote student learning and development that is purposeful and holistic. Programs and services must identify relevant and desirable student learning and development outcomes and provide programs and services that encourage the achievement of those outcomes.**

**Relevant and desirable outcomes include: intellectual growth, effective communication, realistic self-appraisal, enhanced self-esteem, clarified values, career choices, leadership development, healthy behaviors, meaningful interpersonal relationships, independence, collaboration, social responsibility, satisfying and productive lifestyles, appreciation of diversity, spiritual awareness, and achievement of personal and educational goals.**

**Each program and service must provide evidence of its impact on the achievement of student learning and development outcomes.** The table below offers examples of evidence of achievement of student learning and development.

# Frameworks for Assessing Learning and Development Outcomes

| Desirable Student Learning and Development Outcomes | Examples of Achievement |
|---|---|
| **Intellectual growth** | Produces personal and educational goal statements; Employs critical thinking in problem solving; Uses complex information from a variety of sources including personal experience and observation to form a decision or opinion; Obtains a degree; Applies previously understood information and concepts to a new situation or setting; Expresses appreciation for literature, the fine arts, mathematics, sciences, and social sciences |
| **Effective communication** | Writes and speaks coherently and effectively; Writes and speaks after reflection; Able to influence others through writing, speaking or artistic expression; Effectively articulates abstract ideas; Uses appropriate syntax; Makes presentations or gives performances |
| **Enhanced self-esteem** | Shows self-respect and respect for others; Initiates actions toward achievement of goals; Takes reasonable risks; Demonstrates assertive behavior; Functions without need for constant reassurance from others |
| **Realistic self-appraisal** | Articulates personal skills and abilities; Makes decisions and acts in congruence with personal values; Acknowledges personal strengths and weaknesses; Articulates rationale for personal behavior; Seeks feedback from others; Learns from past experiences |
| **Clarified values** | Articulates personal values; Acts in congruence with personal values; Makes decisions that reflect personal values; Demonstrates willingness to scrutinize personal beliefs and values; Identifies personal, work and lifestyle values and explains how they influence decision-making |
| **Career choices** | Articulates career choices based on assessment of interests, values, skills and abilities; Documents knowledge, skills and accomplishments resulting from formal education, work experience, community service and volunteer experiences; Makes the connections between classroom and out-of-classroom learning; Can construct a resume with clear job objectives and evidence of related knowledge, skills and accomplishments; Articulates the characteristics of a preferred work environment; Comprehends the world of work; Takes steps to initiate a job search or seek advanced education |
| **Leadership development** | Articulates leadership philosophy or style; Serves in a leadership position in a student organization; Comprehends the dynamics of a group; Exhibits democratic principles as a leader; Exhibits ability to visualize a group purpose and desired outcomes |
| **Healthy behavior** | Chooses behaviors and environments that promote health and reduce risk; Articulate the relationship between health and wellness and accomplishing life long goals; Exhibits behaviors that advance a healthy community. |

| | |
|---|---|
| **Meaningful interpersonal relationships** | Develops and maintains satisfying interpersonal relationships; Establishes mutually rewarding relationships with friends and colleagues; Listens to and considers others' points of view; Treats others with respect |
| **Independence** | Exhibits self-reliant behaviors; Functions autonomously; Exhibits ability to function interdependently; Accepts supervision as needed; Manages time effectively |
| **Collaboration** | Works cooperatively with others; Seeks the involvement of others; Seeks feedback from others; Contributes to achievement of a group goal; Exhibits effective listening skills |
| **Social responsibility** | Understands and participates in relevant governance systems; Understands, abides by, and participates in the development, maintenance, and/or orderly change of community, social, and legal standards or norms; Appropriately challenges the unfair, unjust, or uncivil behavior of other individuals or groups; Participates in service/volunteer activities |
| **Satisfying and productive lifestyles** | Achieves balance between education, work and leisure time; Articulates and meets goals for work, leisure and education; Overcomes obstacles that hamper goal achievement; Functions on the basis of personal identity, ethical, spiritual and moral values; Articulates long-term goals and objectives |
| **Appreciating diversity** | Understands ones own identity and culture. Seeks involvement with people different from oneself; Seeks involvement in diverse interests; Articulates the advantages and challenges of a diverse society; Challenges appropriately abusive use of stereotypes by others; Understands the impact of diversity on one's own society |
| **Spiritual awareness** | Develops and articulates personal belief system; Understands roles of spirituality in personal and group values and behaviors |
| **Personal and educational goals** | Sets, articulates, and pursues individual goals; Articulates personal and educational goals and objectives; Uses personal and educational goals to guide decisions; Understands the effect of one's personal and education goals on others |

**Programs and services must be (a) intentional, (b) coherent, (c) based on theories and knowledge of learning and human development, (d) reflective of developmental and demographic profiles of the student population, and (e) responsive to needs of individuals, special populations, and communities.**

*Part 3: Leadership*

Effective and ethical leadership is essential to the success of all organizations. Institutions must appoint, position and empower leaders within the administrative structure to accomplish stated missions. Leaders at various levels must be selected on the basis of formal education and training, relevant work experience, personal skills and competencies, relevant professional credentials, as well as potential for promoting learning and development in students, applying effective practices to educational processes, and enhancing institutional effectiveness. Institutions must determine expectations of accountability for leaders and fairly assess their performance.

Leaders of programs and services must exercise authority over resources for which they are responsible to achieve their respective missions.

*Leaders must:*
- articulate a vision for their organization
- set goals and objectives based on the needs and capabilities of the population served
- promote student learning and development
- prescribe and practice ethical behavior
- recruit, select, supervise, and develop others in the organization
- manage financial resources
- coordinate human resources
- plan, budget for, and evaluate personnel and programs
- apply effective practices to educational and administrative processes
- communicate effectively
- initiate collaborative interaction between individuals and agencies that possess legitimate concerns and interests in the functional area

Leaders must identify and find means to address individual, organizational, or environmental conditions that inhibit goal achievement.

Leaders must promote campus environments that result in multiple opportunities for student learning and development.

Leaders must continuously improve programs and services in response to changing needs of students and other constituents, and evolving institutional priorities.

*Part 4: Organization and Management*

Guided by an overarching intent to ensure student learning and development, programs and services must be structured purposefully and managed effectively to achieve stated goals. Evidence of appropriate structure must include current and accessible policies and procedures, written performance expectations for all employees, functional workflow graphics or organizational charts, and clearly stated service delivery expectations.

Evidence of effective management must include use of comprehensive and accurate information for decisions, clear sources and channels of authority, effective communication practices, decision-making and conflict resolution procedures, responsiveness to changing conditions, accountability and evaluation systems, and recognition and reward processes. Programs and services must provide channels within the organization for regular review of administrative policies and procedures.

## Part 5: Human Resources

The program and service must be staffed adequately by individuals qualified to accomplish its mission and goals. Within established guidelines of the institution, programs and services must establish procedures for staff selection, training, and evaluation; set expectations for supervision, and provide appropriate professional development opportunities. The program and service must strive to improve the professional competence and skills of all personnel it employs.

Professional staff members must hold an earned graduate degree in a field relevant to the position they hold or must possess an appropriate combination of educational credentials and related work experience.

Degree or credential-seeking interns must be qualified by enrollment in an appropriate field of study and by relevant experience. These individuals must be trained and supervised adequately by professional staff members holding educational credentials and related work experience appropriate for supervision.

Student employees and volunteers must be carefully selected, trained, supervised, and evaluated. They must be trained on how and when to refer those in need of assistance to qualified staff members and have access to a supervisor for assistance in making these judgments. Student employees and volunteers must be provided clear and precise job descriptions, pre-service training based on assessed needs, and continuing staff development.

Each organizational unit must have technical and support staff members adequate to accomplish its mission. Staff members must be technologically proficient and qualified to perform their job functions, be knowledgeable of ethical and legal uses of technology, and have access to training. The level of staffing and workloads must be adequate and appropriate for program and service demands.

Salary levels and fringe benefits for all staff members must be commensurate with those for comparable positions within the institution, in similar institutions, and in the relevant geographic area.

Programs and services must institute hiring and promotion practices that are fair, inclusive, and non-discriminatory. Programs and services must employ a diverse staff to provide readily identifiable role models for students and to enrich the campus community.

Program and services must create and maintain position descriptions for all staff members and provide regular performance planning and appraisals.

Programs and services must have a system for regular staff evaluation and must provide access to continuing education and professional development opportunities, including in-service training programs and participation in professional conferences and workshops.

## Part 6: Financial Resources

Each program and service must have adequate funding to accomplish its mission and goals. Funding priorities must be determined within the context of the stated mission, goals, objectives and comprehensive analysis of the needs and capabilities of students and the availability of internal or external resources.

Programs and services must demonstrate fiscal responsibility and cost effectiveness consistent with institutional protocols.

## Part 7: Facilities, Technology, and Equipment

Each program and service must have adequate and suitably located facilities, adequate technology, and equipment to support its mission and goals efficiently and effectively. Facilities, technology, and equipment must be evaluated regularly and be in compliance with relevant federal, state, provincial, and local requirements to provide for access, health, safety, and security.

## Part 8: Legal Responsibilities

Staff members must be knowledgeable about and responsive to laws and regulations that relate to their respective responsibilities. Staff members must inform users of programs and services and officials, as appropriate, of legal obligations and limitations including constitutional, statutory, regulatory, and case law; mandatory laws and orders emanating from federal, state/provincial and local governments; and the institution's policies.

Staff members must use reasonable and informed practices to limit the liability exposure of the institution, its officers, employees, and agents. Staff members must be informed about institutional policies regarding personal liability and related insurance coverage options.

The institution must provide access to legal advice for staff members as needed to carry out assigned responsibilities.

The institution must inform staff and students in a timely and systematic fashion about extraordinary or changing legal obligations and potential liabilities.

## Part 9: Equity and Access

Staff members must ensure that services and programs are provided on a fair and equitable basis. Facilities, programs, and services must be accessible. Hours of operation and delivery of and access to programs and services must be responsive to the needs of all students and other constituents. Each program and service must adhere to the spirit and intent of equal opportunity laws.

Programs and services must be open and readily accessible to all students and must not discriminate except where sanctioned by law and institutional policy. Discrimination must be avoided on the bases of age; color; creed; cultural heritage; disability; ethnicity; gender identity; nationality; political affiliation; religious affiliation; sex; sexual orientation; or social, economic, marital, or veteran status.

Consistent with their mission and goals, programs and services must take affirmative action to remedy significant imbalances in student participation and staffing patterns.

As the demographic profiles of campuses change and new instructional delivery methods are introduced, institutions must recognize the needs of students who participate in distance learning for access to programs and services offered on campus. Institutions must provide appropriate services in ways that are accessible to distance learners and assist them in identifying and gaining access to other appropriate services in their geographic region.

*Part 10: Campus and External Relations*

Programs and services must establish, maintain, and promote effective relations with relevant individuals, campus offices, and external agencies.

*Part 11: Diversity*

Within the context of each institution's unique mission, diversity enriches the community and enhances the collegiate experience for all; therefore, programs and services must nurture environments where commonalties and differences among people are recognized and honored.

Programs and services must promote educational experiences that are characterized by open and continuous communication that deepens understanding of one's own identity, culture, and heritage, and that of others. Programs and services must educate and promote respect about commonalties and differences in their historical and cultural contexts.

Programs and services must address the characteristics and needs of a diverse population when establishing and implementing policies and procedures.

*Part 12: Ethics*

All persons involved in the delivery of programs and services must adhere to the highest principles of ethical behavior. Programs and services must develop or adopt and implement appropriate statements of ethical practice. Programs and services must publish these statements and ensure their periodic review by relevant constituencies.

Staff members must ensure that privacy and confidentiality are maintained with respect to all communications and records to the extent that such records are protected under the law and appropriate statements of ethical practice. Information contained in students' education records must not be disclosed without written consent except as allowed by relevant laws and institutional policies. Staff members must disclose to appropriate authorities information judged to be of an emergency nature, especially when the safety of the individual or others is involved, or when otherwise required by institutional policy or relevant law.

All staff members must be aware of and comply with the provisions contained in the institution's human subjects research policy and in other relevant institutional policies addressing ethical practices and confidentiality of research data concerning individuals.

Staff members must recognize and avoid personal conflict of interest or appearance thereof in their transactions with students and others.

Staff members must strive to insure the fair, objective, and impartial treatment of all persons with whom they deal. Staff members must not participate in nor condone any form of harassment that demeans persons or creates an intimidating, hostile, or offensive campus environment.

When handling institutional funds, all staff members must ensure that such funds are managed in accordance with established and responsible accounting procedures and the fiscal policies or processes of the institution.

Staff members must perform their duties within the limits of their training, expertise, and competence. When these limits are exceeded, individuals in need of further assistance must be referred to persons possessing appropriate qualifications.

Staff members must use suitable means to confront and otherwise hold accountable other staff members who exhibit unethical behavior.

Staff members must be knowledgeable about and practice ethical behavior in the use of technology.

*Part 13: Assessment and Evaluation*

**Programs and services must conduct regular assessment and evaluations. Programs and services must employ effective qualitative and quantitative methodologies as appropriate, to determine whether and to what degree the stated mission, goals, and student learning and development outcomes are being met. The process must employ sufficient and sound assessment measures to ensure comprehensiveness. Data collected must include responses from students and other affected constituencies.**

**Programs and services must evaluate periodically how well they complement and enhance the institution's stated mission and educational effectiveness.**

**Results of these evaluations must be used in revising and improving programs and services and in recognizing staff performance.**

All educational materials published by CAS build on the above initially established standards and guidelines that have served as the cornerstone of the CAS approach to self-regulation. From the beginning of CAS, the core function of the consortium was to promulgate professional standards and guidelines, mostly concerned with functional areas in higher education, and to promote their use by practitioners and faculty members in a self-regulatory manner. Thus, self-assessment was introduced by CAS as the primary method of determining program effectiveness and of quality assurance in postsecondary educational programs and services.

Standards and guidelines are structured to include 13 components—mission; program; leadership, organization and management; human resources; financial resources; facilities, technology, and equipment; legal responsibilities; equity and access; campus and external relations; diversity; ethics; and assessment and evaluation. While each set of standards may be used as a stand-alone document for a variety of purposes, leaders of CAS soon realized that practitioners needed assistance in using these standards and guidelines for self-assessment. Acting on this insight, CAS created and published Self-Assessment Guides (SAGs), documents intended to show a step-by-step process for conducting a program self-assessment to determine its effectiveness. Each SAG presents the standards in **bold type** and the guidelines in light-face type and classified the standards into criterion measures reflecting every aspect of the standards, making a ready-to-use assessment tool. SAGs also provide practitioners with a rating scale for each criterion measure. These ratings can be summed to reach a judgment about how well each component of a set of standards and guidelines were met. Narrative guidance also is given about how to use the assessment findings to create an action plan for each program area. Thus, SAGs proved quite helpful to educators carrying out self-assessment activities.

The next major change to CAS educational materials was to add learning development outcomes to the General Standards. This revision was focused primarily on strengthening the program component wherein 16 domains of student learning and development are identified. In this 2003 revision, each domain was illustrated with indicators or examples of relevant learning and development behavior. These examples were intended to assist evaluators by providing several types of student behavior that might be used to structure a formal determination of learning and development that occurred in students as a result of interacting with the various institutional programs and services.

While intended to simplify the evaluation process by providing illustrations of types of behavior that might be assessed, in reality the illustrations exhibited how complicated such an undertaking would be. Thus, CAS leaders foresaw the need for further documents to guide users in the process of determining the extent of domain-oriented student learning and development. The need for further resources to help in this process also was highlighted by the fact that this process moved beyond determining program effectiveness to determining student learning and development within the institution that may or may not be tied directly to a given educational program.

These new educational aids were called *Frameworks for Assessing Learning and Development Outcomes* (FALDOs) and are presented in their entirety in this book. In chapter one, the structure and intent of FALDOs is described in detail. Chapter two calls attention to general assessment considerations, with particular attention to issues of methodology and research design. Finally, in chapters 3-18, all FALDOs are presented sequentially.

# Chapter One

## Introduction

The Council for the Advancement of Standards in Higher Education (CAS) was established for purposes of developing and disseminating standards of professional practice to guide educators in higher education and their institutions in regard to work with college students. Since its inception in 1979, CAS has promulgated standards of professional practice for over 30 functional areas ranging from academic advising to women's programs—service learning programs being a recent addition.

Each functional area plays an important role in the learning process. Therefore, CAS maintains that each program or functional area must incorporate student learning and development in its mission. CAS provides examples of student learning and development outcomes in its general standards that are woven into all functional area standards and guidelines. These examples are associated with 16 learning and development domains identified by CAS including:

1. Intellectual growth
2. Effective communication
3. Enhanced self-esteem
4. Realistic self-appraisal
5. Clarified values
6. Career choices
7. Leadership development
8. Healthy behavior
9. Meaningful interpersonal relationships
10. Independence
11. Collaboration
12. Social responsibility
13. Satisfying and productive lifestyles
14. Appreciating diversity
15. Spiritual awareness
16. Personal and educational goals

Using these learning and development domains in concert with examples of learning and development outcomes, CAS strongly advises all programs and functional areas to incorporate learning and development outcomes in its mission. CAS believes that programs and services must identify relevant and desirable student learning and development outcomes and provide programs and services that encourage the achievement of those outcomes. That is, each program and service must provide evidence of its impact on the achievement of student learning and development outcomes.

It is important to note that CAS promotes self-regulation as the most viable approach to program accountability and learning assessment, calling for each institution to initiate a program of self-assessment for its student support programs and services. CAS encourages program review, learning assessment, and evaluation on a continuing basis using the CAS standards. For this purpose, the Council for the Advancement of Standards in Higher Education publishes *The Book of Professional Standards for Higher Education* periodically and produced the

*Self-Assessment Guides* (SAGs) that include a comprehensive self-assessment process for program evaluation. In addition, CAS presents the frameworks presented herein as a new product for assessing learning in higher education. Each framework is designed as a tool for educators who are concerned about measuring learning and development in college students.

Each framework is organized around one of the 16 learning domains identified by CAS. This is an important distinction between the *Frameworks for Assessing Learning and Development Outcomes* (FALDOs) and the *Self-Assessment Guides* (SAGs). The Self-Assessment Guides are composed of overview questions and criterion measures for each of 13 components of effective educational programs and services including three worksheets to record and analyze findings of effectiveness. Each SAG is associated with a functional area in higher education and includes a worksheet for developing a plan of action to improve the functional area under review.

On the other hand, each framework is organized around a learning domain—for example, intellectual growth, realistic self-appraisal, or leadership development. Frameworks were designed to further enable practitioners to conduct assessment and evaluation procedures that focus on student learning and development. Each framework includes: (a) an introduction, (b) theoretical context for the domain's learning and development, (c) relevant variables and indicators, (d) assessment examples including both quantitative and qualitative methodologies, (e) assessment, evaluation, and research tools available in the public domain, (f) related websites, (g) references, and (h) related materials and recommended readings.

Each framework was designed to emphasize learning and development outcomes over mere satisfaction and program effectiveness. From this perspective, the functional area or program is secondary to its affect on learning. Learning assessment may or may not have specific functional area ties; chances are most professionals will approach their work through the lens of a particular program but it is not essential. Learning is ubiquitous—occurring everywhere at all times. Therefore, student learning and development is neither confined to single program nor institutional effects because education is a much broader concept resulting from all interaction between individuals and their environments.

One purpose of these frameworks is to provide examples of learning and development assessment for practitioners to consider the context of virtually any program or functional area. The point is to give each example character. It is the contention of CAS that learning occurs both within and beyond a specific program and therefore may be assessed without regard to a designated program, service, or functional area. To this end, examples are provided at classroom, program, and institutional levels.

## Theoretical Context

Fundamentally, educators are concerned about learning and development. These phenomena occur in varied ways at different times across all populations. A number of theories have been posited over time to facilitate understanding these processes. For example, psychosocial theory attempts to explain developmental processes such as identity and personality formation. Another line of plausible explanations are often referred to as cognitive-structural theories. The works of Jean Piaget, William Perry, Lawrence Kohlberg, and Carol Gilligan are highly respected benchmarks for investigating cognitive development over the lifespan.

A theoretical discussion is included in each FALDO to highlight the theoretical underpinnings related to a particular domain. For example, in Chapter 2, Perry's work is reviewed to place intellectual learning and development in an appropriate context. Perry posited nine positions associated with intellectual development that represent a movement away from simple, dualistic conceptions of knowledge toward a more diverse and nuanced understanding.

In several domains neither psychosocial nor cognitive-structural theory provides a solid theory base that underlies such learning and development so alternative theories are presented. For example, Chapter 3 presents the framework for assessing learning and development of *Effective Communication*. Given the nature of this outcome, communication theory is discussed in the theoretical context section as it is of greater relevance to learning in this domain than are other theoretical constructs.

## Relevant Variables and Indicators

Due to the fact that a primary purpose of this book is to provide a collection of practical documents, grounded in relevant theory that can prove useful when assessing college student learning and development, each FALDO contains a list of relevant variables and indicators that might be considered in an assessment project. This list is not exhaustive and was designed to provide a starting place for those who need assistance with operationalizing certain constructs. For example, in the spiritual awareness chapter, the list of relevant variables includes searching for meaning/purpose in life, connectedness to others and the world, and religiousness including commitment and engagement. These represent measurable outputs that are closely connected to the outcome.

In general, the relevant variables and indicators are outcomes or specific knowledge, skills, abilities, behaviors, and attitudes expected of college students. Considerable effort and reflection has been given to the list of variables included in each FALDO. For some, the variables were drawn from available research instruments and interview protocols. For others, the variables were discovered from the extant literature and subjected to a thorough review by the editors and advisory committee. In the end, the variables presented in each document should prove useful for measuring learning and development in the domain under question.

## Assessment Examples

A Chinese proverb notes, "Example carries more weight than preaching." This wisdom is relevant to assessment work in higher education. Many people report feeling inadequate or incapable of conducting high-quality professional assessment studies. Some indicate feeling intimidated by the demand for scientific rigor and inferential statistical techniques. In fact, the editors and I presented the concept of our frameworks at several national meetings and our findings were the same. Concerns about using t-tests, stratified sampling methods, and randomized experiments seemed to cover most ears and block out our take home message—good assessment can be accomplished by most professionals.

Our experiences emphasize the importance of and tremendous need for an assessment section of the framework. To be sure, an example carries much weight. But, a modifier may be warranted—a "good" example carries much weight. That is the goal of each assessment example presented.

Following the list of relevant variables, each framework incorporates two assessment examples. The first example demonstrates a way in which *quantitative* methodologies can be used to measure student learning and development within a particular domain. The second example provides an illustration of how *qualitative* methodologies may be employed to assess college impacts on specific outcomes.

In all cases, considerable time and attention were given to identifying the central research/assessment question(s), sample, appropriate tool(s) for data collection, and techniques for data analyses. Every example is framed to be a scenario featuring characters (usually administrators or student affairs professionals) who work at fictitious institutions of higher education. To spice up the readability of this volume and to keep the creative spirit alive, fictitious names related to the learning domain were given to each character. For example, the chapter on *Independence* introduces the reader to Dr. Beema Self (pronounced "Be My Self") who works at Arizona City University. In the chapter on *Meaningful Interpersonal Relationships*, Linda Hand (pronounced "Lend a Hand") at Hewlett University is interested in measuring how college affects students' abilities to establish such relationships with others. All of these steps were taken to give weight to the assessment examples and to make the recommendations for assessment clear.

Gentle reader, keep in mind that these examples are provided to render the complex accomplishable. They serve as metaphors for conducting assessment work and were not designed to be comprehensive. It is hoped that they will provide ample guidance to those who are concerned about student learning outcomes assessment and convince others that assessment can be understood. In addition, virtually every college and university in the United States has an institutional research component, which if approached can often provide technical aid in initiating the assessment process.

## Assessment, Evaluation, and Research Tools

Any good carpenter would agree that before "good work" can be done, good tools are needed. And one would hardly attempt to drive a nail into the wall with only a paperclip in hand. The same philosophy holds true for student outcomes assessment. The quality of any assessment project is directly proportional to the quality of the instrument and techniques used in the study.

With this in mind, each FALDO includes a list of credible research tools that are available in the public domain. In every case, the instrument's full name, acronym, and author(s) are listed. In addition, a short summary of each instrument's purpose follows. The summary may consist of details such as the number of items, subscales, and reliability estimates. Publisher contact information is included for those who may be interested in obtaining copies of the instruments. This section should prove useful when designing assessment projects as it provides a list of several widely used research instruments that purport to measure the developmental phenomenon or outcome under study.

Despite the obvious utility of this section, a word of caution is in order. Do not use this section like you would a *Fingerhut* catalog. *Fingerhut*, a nation-wide direct retailer, encourages its customers to browse-and-shop through its online and print catalogs. Customers can wander aimlessly through each department until they stumble across an item that interests them. Then, using fast credit financing, they can purchase and own the product in seconds! In short, shopping at *Fingerhut* is a speedy process: look, find, like, and buy; the product will be yours to use in a few days.

This is poor wisdom to adopt in assessment work. Assessment requires much more time and should involve a serious period of deliberation, reflection, and thinking. First, think about the purpose of your project and what you hope to learn or discover. Then, think about the type of data you need to satisfy your purpose. For example, if you are interested in measuring the effects of college orientation programs on students' adjustment to college, you need to know among other things: (a) who attended the orientation program and who did not, (b) students' level of adjustment as measured by either an instrument created locally or a research tool available in the public domain, and (c) the other factors that may influence students' adjustment to college so that you can control for compounding effects.

After thinking through these steps, you will be ready to consider your method of data collection. First, remind yourself of the type of data that you need. Then, search for the instrument that will provide you with such information. **Do not do the reverse.** If no instruments yield the kind of data that you are interested in, you are advised to create your own instrument to meet your specific needs. It is also important to note that not all assessment projects require a survey or traditional research tool. In many instances, particularly for qualitative research, an interview protocol, focus group, or semi-structured exercise is an appropriate tool for gathering data.

The take-home point is to stick closely to your objectives. Objectives should be clearly written as they will guide all aspects of your project. They should be reasonable and reflect the essence of your research question(s). All outcomes should be tied to the objective(s). Outcomes must be measurable and related to a specific knowledge, skill, or ability that can be manipulated and observed. Finally, your assessment technique(s) should fit the nature of your objective(s) and outcomes. Tools should be selected that are tailored to your unique purposes and only those that provide the kind of information you need. Remember, good objectives lead to good outcomes, good tools lead to good data, and good data is needed for good analysis. In the end, you get good assessment and good assessment helps people do good work.

## Related Websites

The World Wide Web is a rich source of information today. There are websites devoted to psychosocial theorists (e.g., "Erikson's Tutorial") and even organizational sites for cognitive-structural theorists (e.g., "The Jean Piaget Society" and "The Perry Network"). Usually these websites provide useful information and additional insight into the life of the theorist or interpretation of his/her work.

To make use of these sources, each framework includes a list of related websites that may prove useful to readers. Websites can provide additional material to introduce readers to a particular concept or idea. In addition, several websites are associated with organizations that can provide additional support. All attempts have been made to present a collection of website addresses that function properly.

## References

Most all smart things have been said already; therefore it is necessary to borrow from others when writing a document of this nature. To give credit where credit is due, each FALDO includes a reference section following the guidelines suggested in the American Psychological Association's style manual, 5th Edition.

All references are related to books, articles, and other sources cited in the text of the framework. Only those items that are cited directly in the body of the document are listed in the reference sections. References within the individual FALDO are listed in alphabetical order and are presented at the end of each framework. References for the preface, Chapter 1, and Chapter 2 appear at the end of Chapter Two. References for the epilogue are presented after the epilogue.

### Related Materials and Recommended Readings

Finally, all FALDOs end with a list of related materials and additional recommended readings. This might be expected given the fact that the author and consulting editors are (or were) all faculty members in higher education and student affairs programs. One professor said it best, "All good readings end with more stuff to read." In most cases, this list consists of practical books and articles that relate to the learning outcome featured in the document. In other cases, several journal articles or recent publications are highlighted that shed light on issues related to assessing learning and development in college students. Throughout the book, readers are directed to a number of reference manuals, handbooks, and websites that may contribute to a better understanding of assessment and research.

## Conclusion

There is considerable evidence to suggest that many institutions and programs are experiencing external pressure to provide assessment outcomes that document the contributions of college to student learning and development. Many more report that they do not feel adequately prepared to respond to such demands. Consequently, there is a need for more information and guidance about assessing student learning and development.

To assess growth and change in college, one must know which questions to ask and why, how to interpret or make meaning of the data addressing to those questions, the limitations of the instruments and methods selected, and how to best report findings or results to those concerned. This is the plan, process, and purpose of assessment. I call it the "3 P's." It is also the purpose of this volume—to provide educators with a high-quality set of frameworks for assessing learning and development outcomes (FALDOs).

After serious reflection and heated debate, the author and consulting editors elected to present each FALDO as a stand-alone document. We agreed that the FALDOs would be preceded by introductory chapters that set forth the basic principles and considerations of learning assessment, design, and analysis. We also decided to end the collection with an essay that reemphasized common themes, gathered the loose strands, and acknowledged unanswered questions and issues.

We visualize that the typical user of this volume will read the introductory chapter and then pick and choose FALDOs according to their particular area of interest. We did not assume that every reader would read this book cover-to-cover. For that reason, there is a degree of purposeful redundancy incorporated into the each FALDO presentation in the collection.

We sought to provide, under one cover, a helpful reference manual or handbook for the targeted audience. It is neither a complete nor a final statement, to be sure, and we did not set out to accomplish such an improbable goal. Readers will not find everything they may wish to know about assessment, but will likely find ample material to get started and well on the way to assessing student learning and development outcomes.

This text is about assessment of individuals primarily, not only of student support programs. Many of the examples focus on measuring the influence of collegiate experiences on particular learning outcomes such as spirituality, social responsibility, and leadership.

All of the learning outcomes mentioned can be viewed as goals. These are generally regarded as the proximate goals of college. Proximate goals are accomplished in the short-term while ultimate goals refer to those accomplished in the long-term (e.g., retirement, happiness in life, fulfillment). As previously stated, assessment is about measuring goals and objectives. Therefore, this project was designed to provide guidance about how to measure goal achievement using student learning and development outcomes appropriately. The next chapter focuses on the methodological and technical issues related to assessment and research.

# Chapter Two

## Introduction to Assessment

This chapter is designed to explore the major issues concerning the assessment of college student learning and development. This and other discussions were written for student affairs professionals, senior student affairs officers, assessment coordinators, and interested faculty members among others. The presentation was designed to strike a balance between abstractness and simplicity throughout. The intended audience is anyone who seeks ways to provide credible evidence of student learning and development as a part of institutional self-study, program evaluation, and research.

This discussion is designed to enhance one's understanding of psychometric and design considerations involved in student outcomes assessment. This book provides information for educators to:
(a) Draft a charge/proposal to a committee for the design and implementation of an assessment program.
(b) Measure student learning and development in higher education across 16 learning domains.
(c) Estimate the effects of college on students using measurable learning and development outcomes.
(d) Evaluate the effectiveness of a program or service in higher education and judge effectively the results of an assessment projects' implementation.

This chapter is organized around three major themes: (a) general assessment considerations, (b) technical issues associated with student learning outcomes assessment, and (c) methodological challenges in assessment and research. Specifically, the chapter presents an overview of the assessment process and key components of an assessment plan, technical issues such as internal validity and research design, and methodological and psychometric difficulties concerning the validity of findings.

## General Assessment Considerations

This section focuses on general issues related to assessing learning and development in college students. It serves as an introduction to the sections that follow which emphasize specific technical and methodological issues associated with assessment and research in higher education.

### What is Assessment?

Fundamentally, assessment is linked inextricably to learning and development. In this way, assessment is intrinsic to education (Ewell, 1988). Erwin (1991) defined assessment as "the systematic basis for making inferences about the learning and development of students." He went on to say:

> Assessment is the process of defining, selecting, designing, collecting, analyzing, interpreting, and using information to increase students' learning and development. It includes discussions about what should be assessed and how information will be used, not just the hands-on testing of students. (p. 15)

The two major purposes of assessment are improvement and accountability. Improvement refers to the formative aspects of assessment and evaluation. Accountability, on the other hand, refers to the summative or "effectiveness" dimensions of assessment. Results from formative assessments can be used to improve or reshape programs, policies, or education at large. Findings from summative assessments are typically used to make decisions about the contributions of a program (Erwin, 1991) or in administrative decisions about funding, placement, and restructuring.

Most agree that assessment is here to stay. Increasing demands for accountability and shrinking resources for higher education will raise the need for credible evidence that documents students' learning and development. To collect useful data, researchers must first start with a plan for the assessment project.

### Assessment Plans

While there is no shortage of print materials on assessment, the available literature varies widely in its utility for college educators and student affairs professionals. A number of books highlight recommended frameworks or plans for assessments in business and medical fields, but only relatively recently have assessment texts been available for higher education professionals.

Effective assessment plans have certain characteristics in common. A few of these key concepts are discussed elsewhere in greater detail (Erwin, 1991; Ewell, 1988). For our purpose here, successful assessment plans consists of clear, obtainable goals and objectives; measurable outcomes; meaningful and accurate data; appropriate methods and techniques; and instructions for disseminating results.

Assessment plans refer to the formative aspects of an assessment project. It is during the planning process that objectives are formed and reformed, questions are written and revised, and outcomes are considered. Some refer to this as the strategic planning cycle as it is often the most time-consuming part of the entire assessment project. Remember, assessment planning can be hard work but necessary.

### The Assessment Process

The assessment process, unlike the plan, speaks directly to the "process" of such research; in effect, the procedures and tasks involved in conducting an assessment project designed to measure how college affects students. This also includes the administrative or organizational aspects of assessment work (e.g., delegation, staff support, funding).

Effective assessment projects involve many people in the process (Erwin, 1991). Beyond the assessors and participants, effective assessment projects include internal and external constituent groups such as faculty members, students, and administrators. Additional people allow for additional ideas and may lead to extraordinary work. For example, when studying college impacts, some may contribute student-level knowledge to the group's understanding while others may possess strong assessment or statistical analysis skills. After successful planning of the assessment project, it is necessary to consider how to approach the work.

## Ways of Knowing

Many tend to describe quantitative and qualitative methodologies as if the two were not of a whole (Smith, 1983). While there are significant differences in the underlying assumptions of these two approaches, fundamentally, they represent different ways of knowing or epistemologies. While many continue to place a premium on quantitative research that seeks to explain relationships objectively, there are a number of developmental phenomena that deserve in-depth investigation best fit for qualitative approaches. Creswell (2003) provided the following summary:

| Research Approach | Knowledge Claims | Strategy of Inquiry | Methods |
| --- | --- | --- | --- |
| Quantitative | Post-positivist assumptions | Experimental design | Measuring attitudes, rating behaviors |
| Qualitative | Constructivist assumptions | Ethnographic design | Field observations |
| Qualitative | Emancipatory assumptions | Narrative design | Open-ended interviews |
| Mixed methods | Pragmatic assumptions | Mixed methods designs | Closed-ended measures, open-ended observations |

Source: Creswell, J. W. (2003). Research design: Qualitative, quantitative, and mixed methods approaches (2nd ed.). Thousand Oaks, CA: Sage.

Literature suggests that qualitative approaches such as case study (Manning, 1992a) and naturalistic techniques like (Manning, 1992b), historical inquiry (Schwartz, 1992) are highly effective ways of conducting research. These methodologies have been used in higher education studies, but few employ such techniques to assess college impacts on student learning and development outcomes (Evans, 2001; Evans & Broido, 1999).

Researchers are strongly encouraged to use appropriate qualitative methodologies for the phenomena under investigation. Several criteria may be considered when selecting an appropriate method for data collection. First, based on the research question(s), consider what kind of data would yield results most likely to answer the question. For example, if one is interested in assessing the impact of the first year of college on students' critical thinking skills, one might need "scores" that indicate each student's cognitive ability both before matriculation and at the end of the first year. This suggests the need for quantitative methods such as surveys, aptitude tests, and grades. On the other hand, if one wants to discover the impact of college on students' spirituality, one might consider a qualitative methodology. To investigate this question, one may consider using a grounded theory methodology to analyze interviews or focus groups.

An important distinction should be noted between these two epistemologies. Qualitative methodologies are based on the assumption that knowledge is socially constructed and therefore not wholly describable or controllable (Stage, 1992). Naturalistic forms of inquiry, sometimes also referring to qualitative research, have particular utility for *describing* constructs of interest (Lincoln & Guba, 1985; Stage, 1992; Strauss & Corbin, 1998).

Quantitative research, on the other hand, assigns numbers and symbols (e.g., X, Y) to constructs of interest—also known as variables (Hair, Anderson, Tatham, & Black, 1998). Quantitative methodologies are based on positivistic perspectives that view the world and knowledge as objective and knowable. Under this frame, knowledge can be known in part and ultimately is completely describable and controllable (Stage, 1992).

In sum, many quantitative and qualitative approaches represent different ways of knowing and beliefs about knowledge construction. Each has its own strengths and weaknesses, but both are useful for scientific inquiry. In fact, a number of experts argue that both should be used one with the other to understand more fully the complexities of human existence (Fry, Chantavanich, & Chantavanich, 1981; Smith, 1986; Stage, 1992)

## Technical Issues of Assessment

There are several technical issues related to assessment that deserve attention. These include: (a) reliability and trustworthiness, (b) internal validity and accuracy of data, (c) sampling, and (d) research design. After addressing these important technical issues, the discussion will move on to highlight specific methodological challenges faced by those who conduct assessment research.

### *Reliability and Trustworthiness*

Many people become confused when thinking about reliability and validity and determining which one is which. As a simple rule of thumb, remember that a research tool can be completely reliable yet invalid. Reliability refers to the degree to which an indicator or instrument provides the same information consistently (Neuman, 1994). Here's a classic example: If I weigh myself on the same scale again, and again, and again, and get the same weight each time (assuming that I am not changing my weight by eating, drinking, and so on), then I have a reliable scale. If, however, I get a different weight every time I weigh myself, then the scale is unreliable. While "perfect reliability (and validity) are virtually impossible to achieve" (Neuman, 1994, p. 127), researchers strive to maximize their achievement.

In qualitative research, reliability concerns are often replaced with issues of credibility and dependability (Lincoln & Guba, 1985). In fact, the polemics of the debate switch from the "trinity" (Janesick, 2000, p. 390) of reliability, validity, and generalizability to trustworthiness and accuracy of the data. Trustworthiness refers to the degree to which the qualitative researcher's findings are credible. Peer debriefing, member checking, expert review, and piloting of one's protocol prior to collecting data are several ways to establish trustworthiness (Denzin & Lincoln, 2000; Guba & Lincoln, 1981; Lincoln & Guba, 1985). Peer debriefing is a "process of exposing oneself to a disinterested peer...for the purpose of exploring aspects of the inquiry that might otherwise remain only implicit within the inquirer's mind" (Lincoln & Guba, 1985, p. 308).

In assessment studies that estimate the effects of college on students, it is important to choose or create reliable instruments. This is particularly true for those studies that adopt pretest/posttest or longitudinal designs where the same instrument will be used repeatedly. For if an unreliable instrument is used repeatedly, your assessment is unreliable.

### *Validity and Accuracy of Data*

Validity refers to the extent to which an instrument actually measures what it purports to measure. Neuman (1994) defined validity as "the degree of fit between a construct and indicators of it" (p. 130). Validity is necessay as it determines "whether one can draw meaningful and useful inferences from scores on the instruments" (Creswell, 2003, p. 157).

Given that qualitative approaches seek to understand the particular in depth, when conducted well they give agency back to the particular individual or group being studied. Validity gives way to "accuracy of the data" and steps are taken to ensure that what is being studied is measured accurately. For example, in a study of high quality supervisors, researchers used a form of member checking to enhance the accuracy of data (Arminio & Creamer, 2001). Member checking provides a way for participants to assess the "overall adequacy of the analysis in addition to confirming individual data points" (Lincoln & Guba, 1985, p. 314). Means of determining accuracy of the data are regardless of the approach, important to consider and must be addressed in all assessment and research projects.

### *Sampling*

Sampling is another important consideration in designing research studies. Although in most cases we are interested in the general, it is true that "in science and human affairs alike we lack the resources to study more than a fragment of the phenomena that might advance our knowledge" (Cochran, 1977, p. 318). Therefore, it is imperative that "the fragment" represent the whole. This is the philosophy behind sampling.

Formal sampling is defined as "a process aimed at obtaining a representative portion of some whole, thereby affording valid inferences and generalizations to it" (Cochran, 1977, p. 318). Even in a qualitative sense, sampling is an integral step in the research design process. Though generalizability is not a goal pf qualitative research, sampling must be consistent with inquiry goals.

In quantitative inquiry if the purpose of an assessment project is to study the effect of college on women, the sample and sample size (see Neuman, 1994) must allow the researcher to study a sample of women and generalize the findings to the total population. Studies that focus on the effect of leadership development programs on student leaders should examine this phenomenon using samples of student leaders. While these sampling recommendations seem obvious, there are other nontrivial issues to consider when designing research projects.

### *Research Designs*

The final section of this discussion on technical issues related to assessment focuses on research design. Research design is equally important in qualitative and quantitative inquiry, however Neuman's (1994) work stresses quantitative research design. Qualitative research design is dependent upon the selected methodology. In any case, research design refers to the way in which a researcher organizes his/her study.

Neuman (1994) suggested that an experiment can be framed into seven parts: treatment, dependent variable, pretest, posttest, experimental group, control group, and random assignment. Experiments may not necessarily consist of all seven parts. Typically, researchers combine parts of this framework to shape an experimental design. For example, some studies might omit the pretest and consist of only a treatment and posttest. Others might eliminate the control group and consist of experimental groups entirely.

Several widely used designs have specific names and are cited in the research literature. These include: experimental design or true experiments, pre-experimental designs, quasi-experimental designs, single subject, and factorial designs (Campbell & Stanley, 1963; Neuman, 1994). All subsequent designs are variations of the classical experiment design consisting of random assignment, a pretest and a posttest, an experimental group, and a control group.

Pre-experimental designs "lack random assignment and are compromises or shortcuts" (Neuman, 1994, p. 177). They have shortcomings that make inferring causal relationships difficult. Quasi-experimental designs "help researchers test for causal relationships in a variety of situations where the classical design is difficult or inappropriate" (Neuman, 1994, p. 179). The prefix "quasi" indicates variations of the classical experimental scheme. For more information about such a design, read Campbell and Stanley's 1979 work or Cook and Campbell's treatise (1979).

In student learning outcomes assessment, it is important to consider which design best suits the purposes of one's study. In behavioral sciences, this is crucial as a number of extraneous factors tend to confound essential effects. For example, to study the net effects of college on students' critical thinking skills, it is necessary to assess students' critical thinking abilities prior to college. What is needed is a baseline measure of initial differences in critical thinking for the sample. A good way to design such a study is to use a pretest/posttest design allowing the pretest to serve as a baseline measure of initial differences in students' knowledge, skills, or abilities. Net gains indicated on the posttest, then, can be attributed to the unique effects of college on students (assuming appropriate controls are in place). For more information about using pretest/posttest designs and other technical issues associated with assessment, consult the following studies and texts: Pascarella (2001), Pascarella and Terenzini (2005), Stage (1989), and Terenzini (1989).

## Methodological Challenges in Assessment and Research

Pascarella (2001) pointed out that "estimating the net or unique impact of college on students is one of the most difficult problems in the social sciences" (p. 488). The existing body of college impact studies is fraught with a number of methodological and psychometric problems. These problems present a number of significant challenges that must be considered when one attempts assessment work and college impact studies.

### *Using Statistical Controls*

As previously mentioned, to measure the unique contributions of college on student attitudes and behaviors one must account for initial differences in the sample. A highly recommended way of gathering such baseline data is to use a pretest/posttest design (Pascarella, 2001; Pascarella, Wolniak, & Pierson, 2003). The pretest acts as a pre-intervention measure of the outcome of interest.

However, there may be other factors that confound the effects of college on student learning. For example, insights from previous research studies or theoretical frames may suggest that individual characteristics such as race, gender, age, prior achievement, and/or socioeconomic background exert influence on the outcome variable. In such a case, the researcher must have strong statistical controls in place for student input and/or pre-college characteristics (Pascarella, 2001). Such an approach maximizes internal validity and enhances one's power to draw inferences from results.

*Selecting Data Analysis Techniques*

Within the FALDOs that follow, there are a number of recommendations for suggested data analysis techniques. To maximize the utility of each FALDO, readers are encouraged to consult the statistical methods textbooks and research handbooks cited in the references and recommended readings. In most instances, additional details are needed to analyze data as described in the FALDO.

Generally speaking, there are many ways to analyze quantitative data. To test for differences in frequency distributions, one should consider using Chi-square tests. To explore differences in scores, t-tests are an appropriate analytical technique. And, when groups can be formed, researchers can examine differences in variance of the dependent variable by using analyses of variance (ANOVA) (when studying a single dependent variable) and multiple analyses of variance (MANOVA) for two or more dependent variables.

There are other analytical techniques that are collectively referred to as advanced statistical methods. These include simple linear regression, multiple regression, logistic regression, and general linear models. The main distinction here is the nature of the dependent variable. When the relationship between the dependent variable and an independent variable are linear and direct, linear regression is an appropriate technique. However, multiple regression or ordinary least squares regression (OLS) is the method of choice for analyzing multiple dependent variables or examining the relationship between "multiple" outcome variables and several independents (Pedhazur, 1982).

Logistic regression, in short, is a variation of multiple regression that adjusts for the non-normality of the dependent variable. Logistic regression procedures should be used when the dependent variable is non-continuous—that is, bivariate or dichotomous. A dichotomous variable is best explained as "yes" or "no" conditions. For example, if you are studying the effect of college on persistence, the dependent variable may be whether or not a student persisted—"0" for no and "1" for yes, in most coding schemes. In this case, logistic regression procedures would be used to adjust for the non-continuous, bivariate nature of the outcome (Pedhazur, 1982). General linear models, structural equations, and hierarchical models go beyond the scope of this book. For more information about multilevel models and their application in scientific research, consult the following authoritative sources: (Arnold, 1992; Heck & Thomas, 2000; Hox, 2002; Luke, 2004; Singer & Willet, 2003; Snijders & Bosker, 1999). Though Ethington (1997) provides a more comprehensive discussion on using hierarchical linear modeling in studying college effects, regression is a commonly used technique in research on college students.

Regression is used, generally, for two purposes: (a) to explain relationships between independent and dependent variables, and (b) prediction. In college impact studies, the dependent variable is often the learning outcome of interest. Consider the chapter on *Satisfying and Productive Lifestyles*. The dependent (or criterion) variable may be "satisfied life" or a closely related outcome. Independent (or predictor) variables are those factors that are controlled and manipulated rather than observed. As a general rule, the dependent variable essentially answers the question: What am I measuring? The independent variable is often a grouping variable (for example, gender or year in college) and is the factor that is thought to be causal. For example, in the above referenced chapter, "generativity or giving back" may be one of the independent variables.

## Conclusion

This chapter was designed to introduce readers to the "3 P's" of assessment: the plan, the process, and the purpose. Effective plans consist of attainable goals and objectives, measurable outcomes, appropriate methods, rigorous techniques, and instructions for disseminating results. The process of assessment builds on the plan and aims to involve many people in the project. And, all assessment projects start with a purpose. Generally, the purposes of assessment are improvement and/or accountability.

The second half of the chapter highlighted technical considerations and methodological issues associated with measuring the impacts of college on students. Issues such as reliability/trustworthiness, validity/accuracy of the data, sampling, and research designs must be addressed during the planning process. Methodological issues like statistical controls and choosing a technique are somewhat complex but there are a number of useful handbooks and guides to walk you through the process.

Again, this book is designed to provide guidance to educators and other administrators involved in student learning outcomes assessment. These introductory chapters were written with the entire targeted audience in mind. The remainder of the book consists of 16 frameworks that prove useful for measuring college student learning and development. The final chapter is designed to wrap up the whole process and put it into perspective for those who seek to assess student learning and development.

# References

Arminio, J., & Creamer, D. G. (2001). What supervisors say about quality supervision. *College Student Affairs Journal*, 21(1), 35-44.

Arnold, C. L. (1992). An introduction to hierarchical linear models. *Measurement and Evaluation in Counseling and Development*, 25, 58-90.

Campbell, D. T., & Stanley, J. C. (1963). *Experimental and quasi-experimental designs for research*. Boston: Houghton Mifflin.

Cochran, W. G. (1977). *Sampling techniques* (3rd ed.). New York: John Wiley and Sons.

Cook, T. D., & Campbell, D. T. (1979). *Quasi-experimentation: Design & analysis for field settings*. Chicago: Rand McNally.

Creswell, J. W. (2003). *Research design: Qualitative, quantitative, and mixed methods approaches* (2nd ed.). Thousand Oaks, CA: Sage.

Denzin, N. K., & Lincoln, Y. S. (2000). *Handbook of qualitative research*. Thousand Oaks, CA: Sage.

Erwin, T. D. (1991). *Assessing student learning and development*. San Francisco: Jossey-Bass.

Ethington, C. A. (1997). A hierarchical linear modeling approach to studying college effects. In J. C. Smart (Ed.), *Higher education: Handbook of theory and research* (Vol. 12, pp. 165-194). Edison, NJ: Agathon Press.

Evans, N. J. (2001). The experience of lesbian, gay, and bisexual youths in university communities. In A. R. D'Augelli & C. J. Patterson (Eds.), *Lesbian, gay, and bisexual identities and youth: Psychological perspectives* (pp. 181-198). New York: Oxford University Press.

Evans, N. J., & Broido, E. M. (1999). Coming out in college residence halls: Negotiation, meaning making, challenges, supports. *Journal of College Student Development*, 40, 658-668.

Ewell, P. T. (1988). Outcomes, assessment, and academic improvement: In search of usable knowledge. In J. C. Smart (Ed.), *Higher education: Handbook of theory and research*. New York: Agathon Press.

Fry, G., Chantavanich, S., & Chantavanich, A. (1981). Merging quantitative and qualitative research techniques: Toward a new research paradigm. *Anthropology and Education Quarterly*, 12(2), 145-158.

Guba, E. G., & Lincoln, Y. S. (1981). *Naturalistic evaluation*. Beverly Hills, CA: Sage.

Hair, J. F., Anderson, R. E., Tatham, R. L., & Black, W. C. (1998). *Multivariate data analysis* (5th ed.). Upper Saddle River, NJ: Prentice Hall.

Heck, R. H., & Thomas, S. L. (2000). *An introduction to multilevel modeling techniques*. Mahwah, NJ: Lawrence Erlbaum Associates.

Hox, J. (2002). *Multilevel analysis: Techniques and applications*. Mahwah, NJ: Lawrence Erlbaum Associates.

Janesick, V. J. (2000). The choreography of qualitative research design. In N. K. Denzin & Y. S. Lincoln (Eds.), *Handbook of qualitative research* (2nd ed., pp. 379-400).

Lincoln, Y. S., & Guba, E. G. (1985). *Naturalistic inquiry*. Newbury Park, CA: Sage.

Luke, D. A. (2004). *Multilevel modeling*. Thousand Oaks, CA: Sage.

Manning, K. (1992a). The case study approach. In F. K. Stage (Ed.), *Diverse methods for research and assessment of college students* (pp. 45-56). Washington, DC: American College Personnel Association.

Manning, K. (1992b). The ethnographic interview. In F. K. Stage (Ed.), *Diverse methods for research and assessment of college students* (pp. 91-104). Washington, DC: American College Personnel Association.

Miller, T. K. (Ed.) (2003). *The book of professional standards for higher education*. Washington, DC: Council for the Advancement of Standards in Higher Education.

Neuman, W. L. (1994). *Social research methods: Qualitative and quantitative approaches*. Needham Heights, MA: Allyn and Bacon.

Pascarella, E. T. (2001). Using student self-reported gains to estimate college impact: A cautionary tale. *Journal of College Student Development*, 42, 488-492.

Pascarella, E. T., & Terenzini, P. T. (2005). *How college affects students: A third decade of research*. San Francisco: Jossey-Bass.

Pascarella, E. T., Wolniak, G. C., & Pierson, C. T. (2003). Explaining student growth in college when you don't think you are. *Journal of College Student Development*, 44(1), 122-126.

Pedhazur, E. (1982). *Multiple regression in behavioral research: Explanation and prediction* (2nd ed.). New York: Holt, Rinehart, and Winston.

Schwartz, R. A. (1992). The use of historical methods. In F. K. Stage (Ed.), *Diverse methods for research and assessment of college students* (pp. 57-78). Washington, DC: American College Personnel Association.

Singer, J. D., & Willet, J. B. (2003). *Applied longitudinal data analysis: Modeling change and event occurrence*. New York: Oxford.

Smith, J. K. (1983). Quantitative versus qualitative research: An attempt to clarify the issue. *Educational Researcher*, 12, 6-13.

Smith, M. L. (1986). The whole is greater: Combining qualitative and quantitative approaches in evaluation studies. In D. Williams (Ed.), *Naturalistic evaluation*. San Francisco: Jossey-Bass.

Snijders, T., & Bosker, R. (1999). *Multilevel analysis*. Thousand Oaks, CA: Sage.

Stage, F. K. (1989). College outcomes and student development: Filling the gaps. *Review of Higher Education*, 12(3), 293-304.

Stage, F. K. (1992). The case for flexibility in research and assessment of college students. In F. K. Stage (Ed.), *Diverse methods for research and assessment of college students* (pp. 1-11). Washington, DC: American College Personnel Association.

Strauss, A., & Corbin, J. (1998). *Basics of qualitative research: Techniques and procedures for developing grounded theory* (2nd ed.). Thousand Oaks, CA: Sage.

Terenzini, P. T. (1989). Assessment with open eyes: Pitfalls in studying student outcomes. *Journal of Higher Education*, 60(6), 644-664.

# Career Choices

## A. Introduction

One of the reasons students go to college is to reap employment advantages. Though many educators have negative attitudes toward vocationalism and prefer a broad-based liberal arts education, choosing a career is perhaps one of the most important decisions that we, as educators, help students reach.

Therefore, college students should be exposed to a number of career choices, nurtured to learn about themselves and their interests, and encouraged to make career decisions. Choosing a career is not an isolated event, rather it is about life planning and how lives are spent.

Professional and vocational preparation will continue to be a major outcome of higher education. Making career choices will continue to be increasingly difficult as fields change, technology advances, and the world becomes more global. Therefore, one needs to understand how this development occurs.

## B. Theoretical Contexts for Learning and Development

A number of theorists propose an ecological approach to vocational development (Niles & Harris-Bowlsbey, 2005). By this they mean that career behaviors (such as career choice) are directly related to the quality of interaction between individuals and their environments. This is a well-known scheme in higher education: B = f (P x E)(Behavior is a function of the Person interacting with the Environment). Under this frame, developmental tasks are those required of the individual at each stage of life to master the current social environment and to prepare for the next higher stage of development (Lewin, 1935; 1936; 1951).

Vocational development theory assumes that careers arise, not from a series of isolated and independent decisions, but rather from the complex interweaving of various psychological threads or themes. That is, a pattern of psychological realities gives rise to the events of an individual's vocational life. These events represent the developmental stage and present the individual with a number of developmental tasks or crises. Upon successful resolution of a crisis, the individual gains coping strategies for dealing with such tasks. When developmental tasks associated with one level are resolved, the individual "develops" and moves on to the next higher level. It is important to note, however, that these developmental stages are age-related and will arise regardless of whether the individual has successfully resolved the tasks associated with prior stages (Erickson, 1950; 1963; 1968). In similar fashion, Super's (1957; 1985) theory posits that career decisions are determined by socioeconomic factors, personal abilities, characteristics, and exposure to opportunities over a lifetime.

Vocational development is also connected to awareness of self as worker and understanding of the total person. This is a central theoretical core around which career learning and development can be organized. In this way, career development is interrelated with cognitive development (Perry, 1968) and identity. Some theorists suggest that the complex cognitive tasks associated with making a career choice are beyond the level of cognitive development of many entering college students (Bodden, 1970; Jepson, 1974; Knefelkamp & Slepitza, 1976).

Holland and Lutz's (1967) theory of vocational choice categorizes occupations into six broad types: realistic, intellectual, social, conventional, enterprising, and artistic. Career choices and aspirations are viewed as expressions of "basic personality traits" (Blocher & Rapoza, 1981, p. 216) and self. The college years represent a developmental period in which students can explore career options while juxtaposing their knowledge of self against their growing knowledge of others and work. A number of studies have shown that this theory is useful in understanding changes in career goals among college students (Holland & Gottfredson, 1974; Holland & Whitney, 1968; Krause, 1970; Morrow, 1971). This theory is quite useful in helping people find work that is congruent with their own personality traits.

It is also important to note that much of the research on career development focuses on adolescent, White, middle-class, and vocationally undecided males. There is a growing body of literature on how the process of career development differs for various subgroups of college students. For example, many women struggle with balancing career and family obligations while many older students are challenged with facing midlife career changes (Blocher & Rapoza, 1981). A number of recent studies describe the process of making career decisions as self-authorship or the ability to create an identity independent from but sensitive to social factors, and an ability to consider others' perspectives without being ruled by them (Baxter Magolda, 1999). In short, the stages of development of self-authorship move the individual away from reliance on external factors and an externally defined identity towards an internally generated sense of self (Baxter Magolda, 2001; 2004).

## C. Relevant Variables

- articulates clearly personal values
- communicates personal interests
- has work experience
- comprehends the world of work
- knows the steps of a job search
- describes preferred work environment
- documents knowledge gained
- engages in goal setting

- identifies personal skills and abilities
- able to match personality with job
- engages in volunteer experience
- able to construct resume or vita
- able to write clear job objectives
- ties out-of-class with in-class learning
- has knowledge of various careers and jobs

This list of variables is by no means an all-inclusive list of the relevant variables associated with career development. It is intended to provide a general starting point for thinking about assessing the effectiveness of a program relative to career development. It is important to identify the dependent and independent variables early in the assessment process. The dependent variable essentially answers the question: What am I measuring? The independent variable are the factors that are controlled or vary, often referred to as "treatment." For example, in most cases, the dependent variable might be "ability to make career decisions" while "understanding the world of work" or "able to construct a resume" may be the independent variables.

## D. Assessment Examples

Wanda Work is the Director of Career Services at Avery Community College. In her role, she interacts directly with students and helps them make career decisions by exploring career options, learning more about their interests, and providing assistance during their job search. She teaches two courses, COLL 3210: Career Planning I and COLL 3211: Career Planning II. The courses are designed to provide students with a realistic understanding of various career options, information about their own chosen career fields, opportunities for an internship or externship, and knowledge for launching a job search. However, Wanda was just informed by the Vice President of Student Affairs and the Dean of Students that her classes may be eliminated due to budget reductions. To demonstrate the value of her courses, Wanda decides to conduct a program assessment that emphasizes learning outcomes and considers the following options:

1. Quantitative: Wanda decided to use hypothesis testing as her primary method of analysis. To do this, she wrote three hypotheses that she believes demonstrate the need for and value of the classes: (a) COLL students exhibit a higher degree of self-efficacy and ability relative to the tasks necessary to make career decisions than non-COLL students, (b) COLL students know about more career fields and options than non-COLL students, and (c) COLL students report feeling more prepared for making career decisions than non-COLL students. She used the *Career Decision Self-Efficacy Scale (CDSE)* by Batz and Taylor (2001) to test her first hypothesis. She ordered a single copy of the *Career Interests Inventory* by the Psychological Corporation (1998) and the *Career Decision Scale* by Osipow & Reed (1985) to test the other two hypotheses. Rather than using commercial instruments, Wanda adapted both of these instruments, after receiving permission from the publisher, and created her own to test students' knowledge of career options and their feelings toward searching for a job. Students were asked to pick from a long list of career options to address the question, "What was your career goal when you entered college"? Another question asked students whether or not their career goals had changed during college. Students were also asked to select from a list all of the careers that they knew something about, including job duties, salary information, possible work locations, and education/training requirements. The survey elicited information about how much help students felt they needed to make a career choice.

Wanda administered the CDSE and her own instrument to all students who had taken her career planning classes in the past five years (n=630) and an equal sample of students who had never taken her class (n=630, N=1260). Each student received a score on three subscales: self-efficacy, knowledge of options, and feelings about job searching. Wanda ran an ANOVA to explore differences between the COLL students and non-COLL students.

2. Qualitative: To assess the impact of her classes on students' vocational development, Wanda asked each student to think about career goals and make notes in a journal about how interests changed and how that change affected their career goals and options. Toward the end of the semester, in tape recorded interviews, Wanda asked each student individually about his/her career goals and what learnings from the class were most important. Finally, Wanda asked an open-ended question: How have your career interests and plans changed over the course of this semester? To what degree do you think the class influenced that change? Also, during the interview, students were asked to expound upon their comments in their journals and to clarify any ambiguities. For example, if a student said, "My career interests have become broader," the interviewer asked the student to talk about the careers in which they are interested, and when, where, and how their interests became broader. After the interviews, the tapes were transcribed and Wanda analyzed the transcripts using a phenomenological methodology. She exposed and then interpreted common themes in the transcripts that reflected the lived experience of learning career decision-making skills and traits and when, where, and how skills were developed.

It is worth mentioning that what is being measured here is perhaps the most fundamental purposes of college—insight into self, knowledge, and self-confidence. Moreover, as was mentioned earlier, choosing a career is not an isolated event but rather it is about life planning and deciding how a significant portion of one's life will be spent. Therefore, it is an incredibly important decision.

Due to its importance, professionals may find it necessary or desirous to collect information using a variety of techniques. For example, the qualitative scenario above describes how one might use journaling methods. Still, recent work demonstrates the effectiveness of using electronic portfolios and technology in assessment (Shermis & Daniels, 2002). Practitioners may consider such data collection methods when designing assessment projects.

## E. Available Instruments

A word of caution—be certain that these instruments yield the types of data that are needed to assess the program's effectiveness. To do this, first determine what you want to know and then search for the measurement tool that will provide such information. Do not do the reverse. If none of the available instruments yield the kind of data needed, you are strongly encouraged to develop your own measurement tools to meet your needs.

*Career Decision-Making Survey I & II* by Elizabeth G. Creamer, Peggy S. Meszaros, and Carol J. Burger, 2004.
- Measures attitudes toward technology careers and factors influencing career choices.
- Consists of four sections: personal characteristics, computers and technology, general career questions, and decision making; 99 items and 1 short response.
- For more information: Women in Technology, 211 East Eggleston Hall, Virginia Tech, Blacksburg, VA 24061, or contact Dr. Elizabeth Creamer at creamere@vt.edu.

*Career Decision Scale* by Samuel H. Osipow, Clarke G. Carney, Jane Winer, Barbara Yanico, and Maryanne Koschier, 1985.
- Developed to provide "an estimate of career indecision."
- Publisher: Psychological Assessment Resources, Inc., 16204 N. Florida Avenue, Lutz, FL 33549-8119.
- For more information: www.parinc.com

*Career Development Inventory (CDI)* by Donald E. Super, Albert S. Thomas, Richard H. Lindeman, Jean P. Jordaan, and Roger A. Myers, 1998.
- Measures several affective and cognitive aspects of the earlier stages of career development
- Publisher: Consulting Psychologists Press, Inc., 3803 East Bayshore Road, Palo Alto, CA 94303l.
- For more information: www.cpp-db.com

*Career Decision Self-Efficacy Scale (CDSE)* by Nancy E. Betz and Karen M. Taylor, 2001.
- Measures an individual's degree of belief that he/she can successfully complete tasks necessary to making career decisions.
- Publisher: Nancy E. Betz, Ph.D., 104 Townshend, 1885 Neil Ave Mall, The Ohio State University, Columbus, OH 43210.
- For more information: www.psy.ohio-state.edu/betz

*Career Interests Inventory* by The Psychological Corporation, 1998.
- Designed to assist students in making decisions about their educational and vocational plans.
- Publisher: PsychCorp, Inc., 19500 Bulverde Road, San Antonio, TX 78259.
- For more information: www.PsychCorp.com

*Career Interests Test* by Educational & Industrial Test Services, 1985.
- To determine the relative career interests of young persons and adults.
- Publisher: Educational & Industrial Test Services, Ltd., 83 High Street, Hemel Hempstead, Hertfordshire HP1 3AH, England.
- For more information: www.morrisby.com

*Career Survey* by American College Testing (ACT), 1989.
- To provide students and counselors with information that may be useful for career counseling and to encourage students to consider careers that they may not have considered otherwise. Requires self-reflection and goal setting in order to make short-term educational/career plans.
- Publisher: American College Testing (ACT), 2201 N. Dodge Street, PO Box 168, Iowa City, IA 52243-0168.
- For more information: www.act.org

*Self-Directed Search (SDS)* 4th edition by John L. Holland, Amy B. Powell, and Barbara A. Fritzsche.
- A self-scoring vocational interest inventory designed to match a person's particular activities and interests with various occupational groups.
- Publisher: Psychological Assessment Resources, Inc., 15204 N. Florida Avenue, Lutz, FL 33549-8119.
- For more information: www.parinc.com

*Student Developmental Task and Lifestyle Assessment (SDTLA)* by Roger B. Winston, Jr., Theodore K. Miller, & Diane L. Cooper.
- The Establishing and Clarifying Purpose Task assesses four career choice related subtasks including Educational Involvement, Career Planning, Lifestyle Planning, and Cultural Participation. Publisher: Student Development Associates, Inc. Can be obtained from Appalachian State University.
- For more information: http://www.sdtla.appstate.edu

Several purpose statements were adapted from those produced by the Buros Institute of Mental Measurements Test Reviews Online, www.unl.edu/buros.

## F. Related Websites

| | |
|---|---|
| Occupational Outlook Handbook | http://www.bls.gov/oco/home.htm |
| *Discover* software | http://www.act.org/discover/ |
| Careers in Science and Engineering | http://books.nap.edu/html/careers/ |
| Career Decisions Self-Assessment | http://careerplanning.about.com/od/selfassessment/ |
| Career Development for Meaningful Life | http://www.ericdigests.org/2003-2/career.html |
| Career Development Theory Resources | http://www.ciriello.com/Career/career-development-theory.php |
| Career Planning Online | http://careerplanning.about.com/ |

## G. References

Baxter Magolda, M. B. (1999). *Creating contexts for learning and self-authorship: Constructive-developmental pedagogy.* Nashville, TN: Vanderbilt University Press.

Baxter Magolda, M. B. (2001). *Making their own way: Narratives for transforming higher education to promote self-development.* Sterling, VA: Stylus.

Baxter Magolda, M. B. (2004). Evoluation of a constructivist conceptualization of epistemological reflection. *Educational Psychologist*, 39(1), 31-42.

Blocher, D. H., & Rapoza, R. S. (1981). Professional and vocational preparation. In A. W. Chickering and Associaties (Eds.), *The modern American college* (pp. 212-231). San Francisco: Jossey-Bass.

Bodden, J. L. (1970). Cognitive complexity as a factor in appropriate vocational choice. *Journal of Counseling Psychology*, 17, 364-368.

Erikson, E. H. (1950). *Childhood and society*. New York: Norton.

Erikson, E. H. (1963). *Childhood and society* (2nd ed.). New York: Norton.

Erikson, E. H. (1968). *Identity: Youth and crisis*. New York: Norton.

Holland, J. L., & Gottfredson, G. D. (1974). *Applying a typology to vocational aspirations*. Baltimore: Center for Social Organization of School Reports, Johns Hopkins University.

Holland, J. L., & Lutz, S. W. (1967). *Predicting a student's vocational choice*. Iowa City, IA: American College Testing Program.

Holland, J. L., & Whitney, D. R. (1968). *Changes in the vocational plans of college students: Orderly or random?* ACT Research Report. Iowa City, IA: American College Testing Program.

Jepson, D. A. (1974). The stage construct in career development. *Counseling and Values*, 18, 24-31.

Knefelkamp, L. L., & Slepitza, R. A. (1976). A cognitive-developmental model of career development: An adaptation of the Perry Scheme. *The Counseling Psychologist*, 6, 53-58.

Krause, D. A. (1970). *A study of work values as they relate to Holland's six personal orientations*. New York: Columbia Teachers College.

Lewin, K. (1935). *A dynamic theory of personality*. New York: McGraw-Hill.

Lewin, K. (1936). *Principles of topological psychology*. New York: McGraw-Hill.

Lewin, K. (1951). *Field theory in the social sciences*. New York: Harper & Row.

Morrow, J. M. (1971). A test of Holland's theory of vocational choice. *Journal of Counseling Psychology*, 18, 422-425.

Niles, S. G., & Harris-Bowlsbey, J. (2005). *Career development interventions in the 21st Century* (2nd ed.). Upper Saddle River, NJ: Pearson Education.

Osipow, S. H., & Reed, R. (1985). Decision making style and career indecision in college students. *Journal of Vocational Behavior*, 27, 368-373.

Perry, W. E. (1968). *Forms of intellectual and ethical development in the college years: A scheme*. New York: Holt, Reinhart and Winston.

Shermis, M. D. & Daniels, K. E. (2002). Web applications in assessment. In T. Banta (Ed.), *Building a Scholarship in Assessment*, 148-166.

Super, D. E. (1957). *Vocational development: A framework for research*. New York: Teacher's College Press.

Super, D. E. (1985). Validating a model and a method. *Contemporary Psychology*, 30, 771.

## H. Recommended Reading

Bolles, R. N. (2005). *What color is your parachute 2006? A practical manual for job-hunters and career-changers* (rev. ed.). Berkeley, CA: Ten Speed Press.

Burkett, L., & Ellis, L. (1998). *Finding the career that fits you.* Chicago: Moody.

Edwards, P. & Edwards, S. (1995). *Finding your perfect work.* Itasca, IL: Putnam.

Gilman, C. (1997). *Doing work you love.* Guilford, CT: McGraw-Hill.

Hartung, P. J. (2002). Development through work and play. *Journal of Vocational Behavior, 61,* 424-438.

Herr, E. L., & Cramer, S. H. (1996). *Career guidance and counseling through the lifespan: Systemic approaches* (5th ed.). New York: HarperCollins.

Herr, E. L., & Cramer, S. H., & Niles, S. G. (2004). *Career guidance and counseling through the lifespan: Systemic approaches* (6th ed.). Boston: Allyn & Bacon.

Johnston, S. M. (2001). *The career adventure* (3rd ed.). Boston: Prentice Hall.

Walsh, W. B., & Osipow, S. H. (1988). *Career decisionmaking.* Hillsdale, NJ: Lawrence Erlbaum Associates.

# Collaboration

"I don't like working on teams. I would rather work alone."
—Anonymous college student

## A. Introduction

The legacy of John Dewey's (1916) philosophy on education suggests that genuine learning takes place when education focuses on genuine problems in the community. One of the core problems of society is reflected in the student's comment above. In fact, the underlying personal philosophy of this student runs counter to the attitudes and behaviors that make community possible, namely collaboration.

Collaboration is one of Boyer's guiding principles (Boyer, 1990; McDonald, et al., 2000). He argued that education is intrinsically connected with notions of community and collaboration. Therefore students should be taught in such a way that they learn to collaborate with others in service to community.

Many have pondered the purposes of education and concluded that it has both individual and collective goals. To the individual, education is a process that results in self-development, self-awareness, and personal autonomy among other socially desirable outcomes. It is a personal experience whose ends include promotion of individual welfare and development of personal character. However, education is not exclusively an individual experience because it takes place in a social context that inextricably links the individual to the collective or community.

In this way, a central task of education is to provide a distinctive discipline for membership in a community. Community requires a reasonable balance of independence and interdependence. Therefore, students should leave college being able to work alone and collaborate in group settings.

Collaboration is one of the 16 student learning and development outcome domains identified by the Council for the Advancement of Standards in Higher Education (CAS). An indicator of its achievement includes "working cooperatively with others," for example. Collaboration is related to and sometimes viewed as being synonymous with interpersonal relations, cooperation, and teamwork.

It is expected that all functional area programs will emphasize learning and work to identify relevant learning outcomes. By using CAS functional area standards and guidelines, program leaders can assess student learning and development relative to collaboration.

## B. Theoretical Contexts for Learning and Development

Chickering and Gamson (1987) put forth seven principles for good practice in education. One of these principles suggests that educators should commit to evidence-based practice that uses theory and research to inform practice and scholarship. Therefore, to inform student affairs practice and to assess the effect of college on students' ability to collaborate, one needs evidence. To aid in identifying the kind of evidence needed, one must understand the theoretical basis for learning and development in this domain.

Student development theory is a guide for understanding learning in college. It provides educators with knowledge that can be used to create interventions designed to enhance student learning and development (Evans, Forney, & Guido-Brito, 1998). Developmental theory also provides information about factors contributing to development in cognitive, affective, and behavioral domains such as collaboration.

While there appears to be no discernable theory *on* collaboration, there are a number of hypotheses about collaboration and other closely related outcomes. Collaboration may be one word, but it is related to many things. It is often viewed as synonymous with cooperation, team work, and interpersonal relations. Fundamentally, it is concerned with behaviors such as working with others, balancing levels of independence and interdependence, and cooperating with others in service to a common goal. With this in mind, the work of Lawrence Kohlberg, Arthur Chickering, and Jane Loevinger are important to this discussion.

Kohlberg (1969) focused on the cognitive dimensions of moral reasoning. Advancing the work done by Piaget (1932/1977), Kohlberg set forth three levels of moral reasoning: pre-conventional, conventional, and post-conventional. He suggested that each level of his theory represented a different orientation between the self and society. Essentially, the theory explains development from an individual perspective towards a more universal viewpoint. Collaboration can also be explained as a movement away from independence or "working alone" to interdependence or "working with others."

Chickering (1969) proposed seven vectors of development that lead to establishing identity. His model outlines psychosocial development during the college years (Chickering & Reisser, 1993): developing competence, managing emotions, moving through autonomy toward interdependence, developing mature interpersonal relationships, establishing identity, developing purpose, and developing integrity. Chickering's model is not rigidly sequential and he noted that students tend to progress through these vectors at different rates. Vectors can interact with one another and students often revisit issues associated with vectors they had previously worked through and resolved.

Vectors three and four are closely related to the collaboration domain. During the third, students develop and recognize the importance of their interconnectedness with others. Out of this awareness, students are able to establish mature interpersonal relationships. The tasks associated with vector four include "development of intercultural and interpersonal tolerance and appreciation of differences, as well as the capacity for healthy and lasting intimate relationships with partners and close friends" (Evans, Forney, & Guido-DiBrito, 1998, p. 39). Both tasks involve "the ability to accept individuals for who they are, to respect differences, and to appreciate commonalities" (Reisser, 1995, p. 509).

Loevinger (1976, 1998) took a much more detailed approach and explained this process as ego development. By ego, her model refers to that aspect of personality that assigns meaning to experiences. The term ego development refers to hierarchical interrelated patterns of cognitive, interpersonal, and ethical development that create a cohesive worldview (Weathersby, 1981). Each world view (or stage) represents a qualitatively different way of responding to or making meaning of life experiences. Loevinger's description of the milestone sequences of ego development consists of: impulsive, self-protective, conformist, conscientious-conformist, conscientious, individualistic, autonomous, and integrated. Each transition from a previous stage to the next represents an individual's restructuring of personality. The final stages are marked by the ability to respect others' autonomy and a heightened respect for individuality much akin to the independence/interdependence dichotomy that characterizes learning and development in this domain (Loevinger & Wessler, 1970).

Kegan (1994) created five "orders of consciousness" that takes into account both cognitive and affective components of the lifespan (Evans, 2003). The orders of consciousness range from self-centeredness and a focus on immediate needs to self reflection, and considering the needs and perspectives of others. Then development leads to having a strong sense of identity and evaluating the quality of relationships, and taking steps to enhance them in ways that are beneficial to all individuals. It is from the second to third order of consciousness, between the ages of 12 and 20, where one's own desires can become secondary to the interests of the larger good.

These theories lie at the core of education and reflect a few of the central aims of higher education. They are highly relevant to increased understanding of self, others, and self in relationship to others. In several ways, they relate to one's role as a citizen in a complex, global society and as a member of the classroom community. In either context, it is important for students to learn to work collaboratively and to develop skills that make cooperation possible.

## C. Relevant Variables

- works cooperatively with others
- seeks feedback from others
- exhibits effective listening skills
- establishes mutually rewarding interpersonal relationships with friends and colleagues
- works well in team settings
- exhibits civility and kindness
- seeks the involvement of others
- contributes to achievement of group goals
- establishes and maintains meaningful interpersonal relationships
- treats others with respect
- exhibits necessary balance of independence and interdependence in team settings
- exhibits conscientiousness and self-awareness

This list of variables is by no means an exhaustive list of all of the relevant variables associated with collaboration. Rather, it is intended to provide a point of departure for thinking about assessing the dimensions of learning related to collaboration.

As it is imperative to identify variables early in the assessment process, this list provides the reader with several variables that might be used. As a general rule of thumb, the criterion (or dependent) variable essentially answers the question: What am I measuring? The predictor (or independent) variables, on the other hand, are those factors that are controlled or manipulated rather than observed. The predictor variable is often a grouping variable (for example, gender or year in college) and is the factor that is thought to be causal. For example, in most cases the dependent variable is the learning outcome while "working cooperatively with others" or student involvement may be one of the independent variables.

## D. Assessment Examples

Delvin Taggather is Assistant Coordinator for Student Activities at Vincoat College, a small liberal arts college that has a strong commitment to service-learning and community outreach. He is responsible for the university service-learning center and several programs including study abroad and outreach mentoring. He has a staff of two assistants and a graduate intern.

Recently, Vincoat College has been targeted by the state assembly's new initiative to "reconsider undergraduate education." This initiative was designed to put pressure on colleges and universities to demonstrate what students gain from attending college and how the college contributes to the state's development. In response, a taskforce was established to measure the effects of Vincoat College on students and to identify ways in which Vincoat contributes to the state's needs. Mr. Taggather suggests that several programs and educational opportunities at Vincoat relate to service-learning and community outreach and that collaboration is one central outcome of a Vincoat education. To assess this, the following variables were selected: connection between self and others (self-awareness), awareness of the needs of others (conscientiousness), working with others, and integrity. In this regard, the team considered the following approaches:

1. Quantitative: To test the hypothesis that Vincoat graduates would demonstrate higher levels of collaboration over the course of their college attendance, the team administered the Sentence Completion Test (SCT) (Loevinger & Wessler, 1970; Loevinger, 1996) to three cohorts of entering students. The survey was administered during orientation for the entering classes of 1999, 2000, and 2001. To measure the effects of college on students, each group was surveyed again at graduation in 2003, 2004, 2005 respectively.

   The SCT measures ego development, or operationally for this study: moral development, interpersonal relations, and conceptual complexity (Loevinger, 1998). The SCT correlates answers to open-ended responses such as "My conscience bothers me if..." and "Being with other people..." with seven stages of ego development.

   Data were analyzed using gain scores and ordinary least squares regression controlling for differences in background characteristics and the first SCT score (treating it as a pretest of sorts). After collecting the data, Delvin and two faculty members from the statistics department worked with the graduate assistant to input all scores in SPSS using the scoring manual (Loevinger & Wessler, 1970) for the SCT. Gain scores were computed by calculating the difference between the initial SCT score and the score at graduation. In addition, they ran multiple regression tests to measure the influence of independent variables on the outcome of interest.

2. Qualitative: To assess the impact of attending Vincoat College on collaboration and other outcomes of particular interest to the state, the team decided to implement a new university-wide program. The program required the institution to purchase electronic portfolio software that could be used by all students. After selecting a vendor and having the software installed, all educators were encouraged to incorporate the software in their classrooms and programs. The software was designed to provide students with an electronic portfolio or database where they could store personal documents, activity transcripts, reflective essays, written assignments, and multimedia projects completed during the course of their education.

   Delvin and his staff required all students participating in service learning to reflect on their service experiences through essay writing and to maintain a log of their service projects. These documents became part of each student's electronic portfolio. Methodologists agree that personal documents can yield revealing information (Stage & Manning, 2003; Taylor & Bogdan, 1984). Students were asked to respond to questions such as: What is the importance of community service? How does it connect you to others? What is the meaning of citizenship? In addition, students were directed to keep a written log of their service-learning experiences. Students were encouraged to record their emotions, thoughts, and personal reflections in their logs along with any new information that they learned during the semester. Finally, the culminating assignment was a photography project. Students gathered photos and pictures that related to or reflected their service-learning experiences. Pictures, poetry, magazine clippings, and other visual images were permitted. These images were scanned and became part of the student's portfolio as well. Denzin and Lincoln (2000) suggested that such rich, thick data are useful to understand the meaning of collaboration from the perspective of the actual participant.

Using a narrative methodology, the team used selected portfolios to create a multimedia "story" for the state legislature. Vignettes and reflections were used to demonstrate how students developed over the course of their study at Vincoat College. Likewise, the images were used to demonstrate Vincoat's commitment to service and outreach to citizens and communities in the state.

Regardless of whether quantitative, qualitative, or mixed methods are used, it is important to select an approach that will yield the kind of data needed. When implementing a quantitative approach, one should consider using institutional information previously collected and currently available. In this way, time consuming collection of new data is not required if relevant data are already available. When using a qualitative method, open-ended discussions and self-reports can be useful in collecting valuable data. There are many ways to analyze qualitative data; this is determined by the selected methodology. In any case, this requires a great deal of time and attention. While tools are available, much qualitative data tends to go unanalyzed due to assessors being overwhelmed by the sheer volume of text involved.

It is the intention of this section to render the complex useful; realizing that a degree of accuracy is lost in the process. That is, the examples given in this section of each FALDO are designed to make understanding assessment simpler. It must be remembered that these examples are meant to be descriptive rather than prescriptive about learning assessment. They represent only one way to assess learning and development and definitely are not the only way.

## E. Available Instruments

A word of caution…Be sure that the instruments selected yield the kind of data needed to assess the program's effectiveness. To do this, first, establish what information is essential to the analysis and then select the instrument(s) that will generate such information. The reverse should never be done. If no standardized instruments will yield the kind of data required, it is advised that an instrument be developed that will generate the kind of data needed.

*Styles of Teamwork Inventory (STI)*, Jay Hall, 1995 revised.
- Measures individual feelings about working on team and the attitudes/behaviors one usually demonstrates in team settings.
- Publisher: Teleometrics International, 4567 Lake Shore Drive, Waco, TX 76710,
  Email: info@teleometrics.com, www.teleometrics.com

*Social and Personal Responsibility Scale (SPRS)*, Conrad and Hedin, 1981.
- Assesses dimensions of responsibility along several subscales including attitudes, competence, and efficacy; 21 items
- Publisher: Dan Conrad, Center for Youth Development and Research, University of Minnesota - Twin Cities, Minneapolis, MN 5455-0213

*Team Leadership Practices Inventory (LPI)*, James Kouzes and Barry Posner, 1983.
- Focuses on the behaviors and practices of successful teams and self-guided groups.
- Publisher: Jossey-Bass, A Wiley Company. Instrument was reviewed in the 13th mental measurements yearbook (1998). See review for additional information.

*Measure of Intellectual Development (MID)*, Knefelkamp, 1974.
- Measures the first five Perry positions, 3 essays.
- Publisher: Center for the Study of Intellectual Development, The Perry Network, 1505 Farwell Ct. NW, Olympia, WA 98502, (206) 786-5094

*Measure of Epistemological Reflection (MER)*, Baxter Magolda and Porterfield, 1985.
- Measures the first five Perry positions along 6 domains of the learning process: decision-making, the role of the teacher, the role of the learner, the role of peers, evaluation, and the nature of truth.
- Publisher: Marcia B. Baxter Magolda, Department of Educational Leadership, School of Education, 350 McGuffey Hall, Miami University, Oxford, Ohio 45056, (513) 529-6825

*Moral Judgment Interview (MJI)*, Colby, Kohlberg, Speicher, Hewer, Candee, Gibbs, and Power, 1987.
- Measures moral reasoning in three hypothetical dilemmas using probe questions; structured interview format.
- Publisher: Cambridge University Press, 110 Midland Avenue, Port Chester, NY 10573-4930

*Intra- and Interpersonal Relations Scale (IIPS)* by G. G. Minnaar, n.d.
- Used to identify children's attitudes toward self and parents. Note: Though designed for use with children, it may be adapted for young adults.
- Publisher: Human Sciences Research Council, Private Bag X41, Pretoria, 0001, South Africa, NCWClassen@beauty.hsrc.ac.za
- For more information: www.unl.edu/buros

*Sentence Completion Test (SCT)*, Loevinger, 1996.
- Measures ego development using sentence completions to elicit information about one's frame of reference; 36 items.
- Publisher: Jane Loevinger, Washington University, St. Louis, NO 63130

*Student Developmental Task and Lifestyle Assessment (SDTLA)*, Winston, Miller, and Cooper, 1999.
- Based on Chickering's Seven Vectors, the SDTLA measures college student developmental task achievement including (a) Establishing and Clarifying Purpose (52 items assessing career and lifestyle planning, cultural participation, and educational involvement); (b) Developing Autonomy (52 items measuring emotional, instrumental, and academic autonomy and interdependence); (c) Mature Interpersonal Relationships (42 items assessing tolerance, peer relationships, and salubrious life-style).
- Publisher: Student Development Associates, Inc.
- For more information: www.sdtla.appstate.edu/

Several purpose statements were adapted from those produced by the Buros Institute of Mental Measurements Test Reviews Online, www.unl.edu/buros.

## F. Related Websites

| | |
|---|---|
| National Service-Learning Clearinghouse | http://www.servicelearning.org |
| Center for Effective Collaboration | http://www.air.org/cecp/ |
| Meaningful relationships | http://www.irvingzola.com/rhips.htm |
| Center for Civic Education | http://www.civiced.org |
| Center for Global Partnership | http://www.cgp. org/ |
| Campus Compact | http://www.compact.org |
| AACU-Civic Engagement | http://www.aacu-edu.org/issues/civicengagement/ |
| Teaching Citizenship | http://www.ericfacility.net/databases/ERIC_Digests/ed332929.html |
| Electronic Portfolios | http://eport.iupui.edu |

## G. References

Boyer, E. L. (1990). *Scholarship reconsidered: Priorities of the professoriate.* Princeton, NJ: The Carnegie Foundation for the Advancement of Teaching.

Chickering, A. W. (1969). *Education and identity.* San Francisco: Jossey-Bass.

Chickering, A. W., & Gamson, Z. F. (1987). Seven principles for good practice in undergraduate education. *AAHE Bulletin*, 39(7), 3-7.

Chickering, A. W., & Reisser, L. (1993). *Education and identity* (2nd ed.). San Francisco: Jossey-Bass.

Denzin, N. K., & Lincoln, Y. S. (Eds.). (2000). *Handbook of qualitative research.* Thousand Oaks, CA: Sage.

Dewey, J. (1916). *Democracy and education.* New York: McMillan.

Evans, N. J. (2003). Psychosocial, cognitive, and typological perspectives on student development. In S. R. Komives & D. B. Woodward, Jr. (Eds.) *Student services: A handbook for the profession.* San Francisco: Jossey-Bass.

Evans, N. J., Forney, D. S., & Guido-Brito, F. (1998). *Student development in college: Theory, research, and practice.* San Francisco: Jossey-Bass.

Kegan, R. (1994). *In over our heads: The demands of modern life.* Cambridge, MA: Harvard University Press.

Kohlberg, L. (1969). Stage and sequence: The cognitive developmental approach to socialization. In D. A. Goslin (Ed.), *Handbook of socialization theory and research* (pp. 347-480). Chicago: Randy McNally.

Loevinger, J., & Wessler, R. (1970). *Measuring ego development I: Construction and use of a sentence completion test* (Vol. 1). San Francisco: Jossey-Bass.

Loevinger, J. (1976). *Ego development: Conceptions and theories.* San Francisco: Jossey-Bass.

Loevinger, J. (1996). Meaning and measurement of ego development. *American Psychologist*, 21, 195-206.

Loevinger, J. (1998). History of the Sentence Completion Test (SCT) for ego development. In Loevinger, J. (Ed.) *Technical foundations for measuring ego development: The Washington University Sentence Completion Test.* Mahwah, NJ: Lawrence Erlbaum Associates.

McDonald, W. M., Bacon, J. L., Brown, C. E., Carter, A. W., Littleton, R. A., Moore, B. L., Roper, L. D., & Tankersley, E. (2000). *Collaboration and community: Boyer's guiding principles.* Washington, DC: NASPA.

Piaget, J. (1977). *The moral judgment of the child* (M. Gabain, Trans.). Hardmondsworth, England: Penguin. (Original work published 1932)

Reisser, L. (1995). Revisiting the seven vectors. *Journal of College Student Development,* 36, 505-511.

Stage, F. K., & Manning, K. (2003). *Research in the college context: Approaches and methods.* New York: Brunner-Routledge.

Taylor, S. J., & Bogdan, R. (1984). *Introduction to qualitative research methods: The search for meanings.* New York: John Wiley & Sons.

Weathersby, R. P. (1981). Ego development. In A. W. Chickering & Associates (Eds.), *The modern American college: Responding to the new realities of diverse students and a changing society* (pp. 51-75). San Francisco: Jossey-Bass.

## H. Recommended Reading

Chirban, J. T. (2004). *True coming of age: A dynamic process that leads to emotional stability, spiritual growth, and meaningful relationships.* New York: McGraw-Hill.

Duck, S. (1994). *Meaningful relationships: Talking, sense, and relating.* Thousand Oaks, CA: Sage.

Erlich, T. (2000). *Civic responsibility and higher education.* Phoenix, AZ: Oryx Press.

Maloney, W. A. (2000). The community as classroom. *Academe,* 86(4), 38-42.

Zlotkowski, E. (1996). Linking service-learning and the academy. Change, 28, 21-27.

Upcraft, M. L, & Schuh, J. H. (1996). *Assessment in student affairs: A guide for practitioners.* San Francisco: Jossey-Bass.

Upcraft, M. L., & Schuh, J. H. (2000). *Assessment practice in student affairs: An applications manual.* San Francisco: Jossey-Bass.

# Effective Communication

## A. Introduction

The Oxford English Dictionary defines communication as "the imparting, conveying, or exchange of ideas, knowledge, and information." This is useful when defining a learning domain such as effective communication. Effective communication is one of the learning and development outcomes identified by the Council for the Advancement of Standards in Higher Education (CAS). It is related to verbal competence and other academic skills such as listening and writing. Indicators of its achievement include writing and speaking coherently and effectively, to name a few.

Communication is a word with a long, rich history. It entered the English language in the 14th and 15th centuries (Mattelart, 1996). Derived from the Latin *communicare*, the word means to share or make common. It is closely related to other words derived from its Latin root. Such words include: meaning, common, and community.

A number of scholars agree that communication is fundamental and necessary for understanding, living with, and learning from others (Dewey, 1938). In this way, effective communication is not only an appropriate outcome of college learning but is a vital skill through which learning and development are facilitated. Learning to communicate effectively has been shown to improve one's grades (Astin & Astin, 1993), test scores (Smith, 1992), and the college experience in general (Arnold, Kuh, Vesper, & Schuh, 1991; Kuh, Pace, & Vesper, 1997).

The benefits of learning to communicate effectively are important for education and the preservation of society. The costs of not communicating are rife with negative consequences and run counter to the purposes of education. Sayers and Madden (1959) suggested that "not communicating with one another" or communicating poorly breeds "mutual distrust, hostility, and fear" (p. 254). They went on to state, "We are silent because we are afraid we cannot discuss...matters in a manner worthy of men [sic], but our silence breeds an unhealthy atmosphere contributing to fear itself" (p. 254). While this is likely true, we know from work done by Belenky, Clinchy, Goldberger, and Tarule (1986) and Goldberger, Tarule, Clinchy, and Belenky (1996) that some people are silenced by oppression and violence, some are silent because they have not learned how to give voice to who they are, and others choose silence as a strategy to avoid retribution. In any case, lack of communication or poor communication begets fear and fear stands in the way of learning, development, and community.

As Dewey (1938) stated, education is experience. While in college, students experience a myriad of personal interactions with faculty, staff, and other students. College students also experience various learning environments and opportunities for development; often influenced by the individual student's learning style. All of these experiences are educative and should promote the achievement of various outcomes such as effective communication.

## B. Theoretical Contexts for Learning and Development

There exists a large body of theoretical constructs related to communication usually referred to as communication theory. Communication theory suggests that communication is an exchange or transaction between a sender and a receiver. The sender is the source of information while the receiver is responsible for decoding, reconstructing, and interpreting the sender's message. Effective communication, then, is related to the degree to which the original sender's message matches the receiver's interpretation.

Notable communication theorists include Peirce (1898), Rogers (1994), and Shannon (McMillan, 1994). Peirce studied the sign systems and modes that humans use to express feelings, thoughts, and ideas. This is referred to as semiotics. Rogers emphasized the importance of dialogue or two-way communication. He believed that mutual understanding leads to freedom.

Shannon is cited frequently as a theorist of human communication. He posited that communication consists of a sender, a transmission medium, and a receiver. Shannon was among the first to include a measure of the amount of information in a message. The importance of a message, in his mind, is related to the predictability of the message. That is, if one can easily predict the content of a message, then the message has little information and is of little importance. But, if the message consists of information that is unpredictable, it has a large amount of information and is important.

In this way, effective communication is the successful transmission of information from a sender to a receiver through a medium (e.g., speech, writing, art form, sign language, etc.). Communication is effective and optimal when the message is of importance and contains a measure of information. In short, effective communication begins when one has something important to convey. Then, the sender must transmit the message to others using an appropriate method of communication.

By understanding the theoretical context of effective communication, educators not only gain an appreciation for the contributions of communication but also unpack the meaning of communication as an exchange of information. With such knowledge, practitioners and teachers are able to assess learning and development in this area using appropriate measures.

## C. Relevant Variables

- writes coherently
- influences others through the written word
- expresses thoughts and emotions through writing
- articulates abstract ideas
- writes essays or personal letters
- writes in an organized fashion
- communicates in non-traditional forms (e.g., email, performance, body language)

- speaks effectively
- influences others through the spoken word
- expresses thoughts and emotions through speaking
- uses appropriate syntax
- presents orally
- speaks in logical and orderly terms
- moves from general topics to specific topics in writing and speech

This list of variables is by no means an exhaustive list of all of the relevant variables associated with effective communication. Rather, it is intended to provide a point of departure for thinking about assessing the dimensions of learning related to effective communication. It should also be noted that although the words "say" and "write" are used here, due to physical and learning limitations, people use other forms of communication to convey their ideas such sign language and voice generated computers.

As it is imperative to identify variables early in the assessment process, this list provides the reader with several relevant variables that might be used. As a general rule, the criterion (or dependent) variable essentially answers the question: "What am I measuring?" The predictor (or independent) variables, on the other hand, are those factors that are controlled or manipulated rather than observed. The predictor variable is often a grouping variable (for example, gender or year in college) and is the factor that is thought to be causal. For example, in most cases the dependent variable is the learning outcome (e.g., effective communication) while "ability to write essays" may be one of the independent variables.

## D. Assessment Examples

Chat N. Wright is the Coordinator of Academic Enrichment at Hill Springs College. In this position, he provides academic advising to undergraduate students in all majors and works along with faculty members to meet the academic needs of under-prepared and under-represented students. He was recently assigned to the institution's "Effects of College Taskforce," chaired by the Director of Institutional Effectiveness. One of their purposes is to assess how much students learn during the college years across several learning domains. They adopted several of the learning domains identified by CAS including Effective Communication. To measure the effect of college on students' communication skills, the team considered the following two approaches:

1. Quantitative: To measure the gains associated with attending college relative to communication skills, Mr. Wright and members of the taskforce administered the *College Basic Academic Subjects Examination (CBASE)* to a sample of 500 students in October of their first year. Then, the team re-tested the same sample with the same instrument in May of their second year. A second follow-up using the same sample and instrument occurred in May of their fourth year. Using the score on each of the four subscales (e.g., English, math, science, and social studies), the researchers calculated gain scores to compare how much was learned between years one and two and between years one and four.

2. Qualitative: To measure the gains associated with attending college using a qualitative methodology, the researchers selected ethnography, or the study of culture, to assess effective communication skills of students. Specifically, the task force members decided to focus on students' ability to influence others through written word, spoken word; and, the ability to express thoughts and emotions through writing and speaking. Ten members of the task force were trained by an ethnographer from the anthropology department on ethnography as a qualitative research methodology, and observation and document review as means of collecting data. Along with the ethnographer, the task force members decided on aspects of the campus they would observe over the course of the semester. They included examples of oral communication such as class discussions and presentations, student radio productions, student government meetings, spontaneous interactions, and interactions in the dining hall. They also read documents prepared by students including the student newspaper, yearbook, sample papers, and websites.

Through their strategic observations and document review, task force members noted the quality in which students are able to accomplish the above tasks and how the quality of tasks changed over the course of a semester. They noted commonalities of their observations but also unique findings always seeking to gain rich and in depth insight into student communication skills.

## E. Available Instruments

A word of caution—be certain that the instruments selected yield the type of data needed to answer your assessment question. To do this, first determine what you want to know and then search for the instrument that will provide such information. Do not do the reverse. If no standardized instrument can yield the kind of data in which you are interested, you are advised to create your own instrument to meet your specific needs.

*College Basic Academic Subjects Examination (CBASE)* by Osterlind, n.d.
- Standardized, criterion-referenced achievement test designed to measure the degree to which students have mastered particular skills and competencies related to general education coursework.
- Publisher: Assessment Resource Center, University of Missouri-Columbia, College of Education, 2800 Maguire Blvd., Columbia, MO 65211.
- For more information: www.arc.missouri.edu; www.unl.edu/buros/

*College Outcome Measures Program (COMP)* by ACT, Inc., n.d.
- Standardized test designed to assess "liberal arts" learning and skills including science, using art, and solving problems.
- Publisher: ACT, Inc., 2201 N. Dodge Street, PO Box 168, Iowa City, IA 52243.
- For more information: www.act.org; www.unl.edu/buros/

*Collegiate Assessment of Academic Proficiency (CAAP)* by ACT, Inc., n.d.
- 35-item math assessment designed to measure students' ability to solve mathematical problems associated with college curricula.
- Publisher: ACT Inc., 2201 N. Dodge Street, P. O. Box 168, Iowa City, IA 52243.
- For more information: www.act.org; www.unl.edu/buros/

Several purpose statements were adapted from those produced by the Buros Institute of Mental Measurements Test Reviews Online, www.unl.edu/buros.

## F. Related Websites

| | |
|---|---|
| *Oxford Journal of Communication Theory* | www.ct.oupjournals.org |
| Communication theory | www.uiowa.edu/~journal/publications/iccs.html |
| Theory of communication | www.carbon.cudenver.edu/~mryder/itc/comm._theory.html |
| Theory archives | www.afirstlook.com/archther.cfm |
| Meta-discourses Theory | www.colorado.edu/communication/meta-discourses/index.htm |
| Technical Communications Group | http://suman_malik.tripod.com/tcg/id10.html |
| Writing Skills Guide | www.infoplease.com/homework/writingskills1.html |
| How to Write Right | www.see.ed.ac.uk/~gerard/management/art4.html |
| The World of Writing | www.bloorstreet.com/300block/3author.htm |
| Harvard's Writing Lab | www.fas.harvard.edu/~expos/project.cgi?section |

## G. References

Arnold, J., Kuh, G., Vesper, N., & Schuh, J. (1991, November). *The influence of student effort, college environment, and selected student characteristics on undergraduate student learning and personal development at metropolitan institutions.* Paper presented at the meeting of the Association for the Study of Higher Education, Boston.

Astin, A., & Astin, H. (1993). *Undergraduate science education: The impact of different college environments on the educational pipeline in the sciences.* Los Angeles: University of California, Graduate School of Education, Higher Education Research Institute.

Belenky, M. F., Clinchy, B. M., Goldberger, N. R., & Tarule, J. M. (1986). *Women's way of knowing: The development of self, voice, and mind.* New York: Basic Books.

Dewey, J. (1938). *Experience and education.* New York: Touchstone Books.

Goldberger, N., Tarule, J., Clinchy, B., & Belenky, M. (Eds.). (1996). *Knowledge, difference, and power Essays inspired by Women's Ways of Knowing.* New York: Basic Books.

Kuh, G., Pace, C., & Vesper, N. (1997). The development of process indicators to estimate student gains associated with good practices in undergraduate education. *Research in Higher Education*, 38, 435-454.

Mattelart, A. (1996). *The invention of communication* (S. Emanuel, Trans.). Minneapolis: University of Minnesota Press.

McMillan, B. (1994). *Scientific impact of the work of Claude E. Shannon.* Proceedings of the Norbert Wiener Centenary Congress. East Lansing, MI.

Peirce, C. S. (1898). Logic as semiotic: The theory of signs. In J. Bucher (Ed.), *Philosophical writing of Peirce.* New York: Dover.

Rogers, C. (1994). The necessary and sufficient conditions of therapeutic personality change. In R. Anderson, K. N. Cissna, & R. C. Arnett (Eds.), *The reach of dialogue: Confirmation, voice, and community* (pp. 126-140). Cresskill, NJ: Hampton Press. (Original work published 1957.)

Sayers, E. V., & Madden, W. (1959). *Education and the democratic faith: An introduction to philosophy of education.* New York: Appleton-Century-Crofts, Inc.

Smith, K. (1992). Gender differences and the impact of college on White students' racial attitudes. *Dissertation Abstracts International*, 53, 3819A.

## H. Recommended Reading

Berlo, D. K., & Reiser, R. A. (1987). Instructional technology: A history. In R. M. Gagné (Ed.). *Instructional technology: Foundations* (p. 16). Hillsdale, NJ: Erlbaum.

Cameron, D. (2000). *Good to talk? Living and working in a communication culture.* London, UK: Sage.

Carey, J. W. (1989). *Communication as culture: Essays on media and society.* Winchester, MA: Unwin Hyman.

Craig, R. T. (1999). Communication theory as a field. *Communication Theory*, 9(2), 199-161.

McKeon, R. (1957). Communication, truth, and society. *Ethics*, 67, 89-99.

McLuhan, M. (1998). *Understanding media: The extensions of man.* Cambridge, MA: The Massachusetts Institute of Technology Press.

Penman, R. (2000). *Reconstructing communicating: Looking to a future.* Mahwah, NJ: Lawrence Erlbaum.

Perkins, B. D. (2000, September 1). Wilbur Schramm overview. University of North Carolina. Retrieved March 25, 2001, from http://www.cultsock.ndirect.co.uk/MUHome/cshtml/introductory/schro1.html.

Peters, J. D. (1999). *Speaking into the air: A history of the idea of communication.* Chicago: University of Chicago Press.

Rogers, E. M. (1994). *A history of communication study: A biographical approach.* New York: Free Press.

Schiller, D. (1996). *Theorizing communication: A history.* New York: Oxford University Press.

# Appreciating Diversity

## A. Introduction

The beginning point of this discussion lies in the recognition that diversity matters. It is almost certain that individuals from different cultures or of different genders perceive the world differently (Bean & Eaton, 2000). Different perspectives often lead to innovation, improvement of old processes, and development. In fact, scholars agree that the future of the nation and the preservation of a democratic society are tied to an educated diverse citizenry. Higher education has a vital role to play, both as a force of social justice and in producing an educated and productive citizenry. To this end, educators must ensure that students are taught to competently work in diverse environments and value diverse cultures.

A report of the Commission on Minority Participation in Education and American Life (1988) titled, "One-Third of a Nation," indicated that "America is moving backward—not forward—in its effort to achieve the full participation of minority citizens in the life and prosperity of the nation" (p. 3). The commission called for all segments and members of society to overcome "the current inertia and remove the remaining barriers to full participation of education and in all other aspects of American life" (p. 5). Roughly two decades later, America is still struggling to achieve equal opportunity and access to education for all members of its society.

Recent reports suggest that there has been substantial improvement in increasing the number of African Americans, Hispanics, and other underrepresented groups in higher education institutions, but a number of caveats are in order. For example, the *Chronicle of Higher Education* provided information that "while 64% of full-time students at four-year colleges graduate within six years, less than half of all Black and Hispanic students do so in that period of time. The rates from low-income families are only slightly better" (Burd, 2004, p. A19). The same article reported that differences in graduation rates between Hispanic and White students are seven to fifteen percentage points higher at one fourth of all four-year institutions. Other reports highlight the fact that improvement in increasing the numbers does not translate into equal representation. Schmidt (2003) reported that though Michigan is 14.2% Black, only 7.8% of the college enrollment is Black.

To be sure, there is still much to be done. In higher education, one cannot accept anything less than creating truly pluralistic campus communities. To become truly reflective of the pluralism of American life, one must examine the dominant assumptions, structures, and priorities that guide behavior. This point of view represents a redress of the status quo and moves diversity away from mere tolerance towards acceptance and appreciation. It is not enough to simply welcome "other" individuals into one's culture. Diversity requires systemic change in the institution's culture so that all members of the community feel valued, experience a sense of belonging, and honor each other's differences.

Diversity in the higher education context is significantly related to campus climate. Campus climate, or environment (Bean & Eaton, 2000), refers to the physical setting, organizational factors, common characteristics, and social climate of colleges and universities. Students' personal interpretations of their institutions' climates—that is, the opportunities and challenges—shape their behaviors. For students to truly appreciate diversity, the campus climate must foster a sense of awareness, appreciation, and understanding of the differences in and contributions of others.

Many institutions have sought diligently to make their campuses truly reflective of the rich diversity of the host country. For example, a research university in the northeast United States increased participation in the developmental studies program by 50% to improve recruitment and retention of underrepresented students. Another institution heeded national data indicating that students of color tend to score lower on the SAT than do White students. Consequently, they incorporated nontraditional measures in their admissions evaluation procedures. This change provided counselors with new information to make more informed decisions based on the student's academic and non-academic interests, involvement, and characteristics. This approach is highly recommended in Sedlacek's (2004) *Beyond the Big Test.*

In summary, diversity matters. But, the benefits of diversity are not without cost. The costs of change include time, energy, will, and funds. Yet, such hard work is no excuse for retreat. In the words of Judith Eaton, President of the Council for Higher Education Accreditation, "We cannot resign…. The injustice is too great for a democratic nation to condone; the costs are too high for all citizens" (Green, 1989, p. vii). This implies that there is reciprocity to diversity. That is, when one engages with someone else, both benefit. Therefore, diversity should be embraced by all in all forms and at all levels.

More recent works demonstrate the educational benefits of diversity. Bowen and Bok (1998) provided a wealth of evidence that graduates of selective diverse institutions value educational diversity, support race-sensitive admissions, and have experiences in interacting across racial lines. Talbot (2003) highlighted a number of sources that detail the effect of studying in a diverse environment on self-confidence, critical thinking, and greater involvement in civic and community service. In detailing the learning benefits of diverse students, Blimling (2001) succinctly stated, "diversity makes you smarter" (p. 518).

Finally, a word about language. Diversity is an emotionally charged and value-laden topic. In some ways, it has become a benign buzzword of the academy that conjures up images of fire-side chats about humankind's unity. For others, the term connotes affirmative action, quotas, discrimination, and racism. These all point to the perceptions of diversity's meanings and implications. For the purposes of this framework, diversity refers to valuing aesthetics, culture, and social identity differences.

Pluralism and diversity are related terms. In a report issued by Brown University, *The American University and the Pluralist Ideal* (1986), the term "diversity" was used to connote "the mere presence of multiple ethnic and racial groups within the community" (p. 5). Pluralism has to some a more positive and active connotation, whereas it "asks of the members of all groups to explore, understand, and try to appreciate one another's cultural experiences and heritage" (p. 5). Some would argue that diversity implies passive coexistence while pluralism refers to a dynamic atmosphere of collaboration. The authors of this Framework have chosen to use the two terms interchangeably, with the meanings above ascribed to both.

## B. Theoretical Contexts for Learning and Development

Explaining diversity is an enormously complex enterprise where no single theory of development has dominance in the field. In fact, there is little agreement over the definition of diversity and how its appreciation is best measured. I believe it is important to make a distinction between two types of diversity: what I refer to as, diversity-in-kind and diversity-in-mind.

When most people think of diversity, they think of diversity-in-kind. This refers to the coexistence and appreciation of people from various backgrounds, racial/ethnic groups, and cultures. It implies a mix of genders, physical characteristics, and sexual orientations. Diversity involves race, color, religion, gender, national origin, physical or mental handicap, age, veteran status, sexual orientation, and intellectual capacity.

Diversity-in-mind, on the other hand, refers to the multiplicity of viewpoints and opinions often referred to as the multiplicity of thought. As stated earlier, individuals from different cultures or of different genders perceive the world differently. This leads to alternative worldviews and varying frames of reference. Diversity, in this sense, suggests that all informed viewpoints are valuable and should be honored and appreciated within reason. In fact, the philosophy of diversity assumes that each logical view or frame is given equal weight, time, and attention. I believe diversity-in-mind is more ideological while diversity-in-kind is more philosophical.

Theoretically, diversity-in-kind relates to psychosocial theory, especially identity development. Chickering (1969) proposed seven vectors of development that contribute to the formation of identity. He used the term vector to imply both magnitude and direction because each served as a "major highway for journeying toward individuation" (Chickering & Reisser, 1993, p. 35). The seven vectors presented in his revised theory are: (1) developing competence, (2) managing emotions, (3) moving through autonomy toward interdependence, (4) developing mature interpersonal relationships, (5) establishing identity, (6) developing purpose, and (7) developing integrity. However, there is evidence that Chickering's vectors do not adequately address the identity development of traditionally under-represented students (Evans, Forney, Guido- Brito, 1998). Since 1969, there have been a number of identity development models created to better understand identity development of various groups. These include Cross (1971, 1978), D' Augelli (1991), Helms (1995), Phinney (1989), and Torres (1999), among others.

Chickering's fourth and fifth vectors are closely related to diversity-in-kind. The developing mature relationships vector acknowledges that experiences with relationships contribute significantly to the development of a sense of self. The tasks associated with this vector include "development of intercultural and interpersonal tolerance and appreciation of differences, as well as the capacity for healthy and lasting intimate relationships with partners and close friends" (Evans, Forney, & Guido-DiBrito, 1998, p. 39). The fifth vector acknowledges differences based on gender, ethnic background, and sexual orientation. Identity involves comfort and acceptance of one's self as well as understanding and appreciation of others.

There are also a number of diversity development models that are directly related to this domain. Pedersen (1988) posited a Multicultural Development Model consisting of awareness, knowledge, and skills. Bennett (1986) set forth a Development of Intercultural Sensitivity Model that relates to training for diversity. Still, there is exciting work in the area of social justice ally development. Broido (2000) and Reason, Roosa Millar, and Scales (2005) have contributed new theoretical knowledge to this area.

Simply put, diversity-in-mind or multiplicity of thought is associated with increasing levels of cognitive complexity. That is, development of this sort refers to changes in the cognitive structures of an individual. It is characterized by a movement away from simple, bimodal understandings toward more complex forms of integration and differentiation.

The works of Piaget (1950; 1952), the father of cognitive-structural developmental theories, Perry (1968; 1978; 1981); and Kitchener and King (1981) are important and relevant to this domain. These theories are referred to as cognitive-structural theories (see *Intellectual Development FALDO*). Cognitive structural theories focus on changes in the way people think rather than the *content* or substance of their thinking. For example Perry's theory relates to meaning making processes and consists of nine positions that can be grouped into four categories: (1) dualism, (2) multiplicity, (3) relativism, and (4) commitment. His theory is characterized by a

# Frameworks for Assessing Learning and Development Outcomes

logical progression from simple meanings to more complex modes of reasoning or multiplicities of thought. Duality suggests that one right answer exists for everything while multiplicity acknowledges diverse views.

By understanding psychosocial theory, educators can better understand "kind differences" related to identity and relationships. Cognitive-structural theory may be used to understand "mind differences" or differences in the *way* people think. With such knowledge, educators can be more intentional in providing instruction and services that promote appreciation of diversity.

## C. Relevant Variables

- accepts others
- understands others culture
- seeks involvement with people different from oneself
- articulates the advantages of a diverse society
- challenges appropriately the use of stereotypes by others
- develops appreciation for art, music, and forms of expression by others perspectives

- defines diversity accurately in ones' own words
- employs complex reasoning
- understands ones own identity
- understands ones own culture
- seeks involvement in different interests and activities
- articulates the challenges to a diverse society
- understands the impact of diversity on one's own society
- appreciates the presence of different viewpoints and
- defines pluralism accurately in ones' own words

This list of variables is by no means an exhaustive list of all of the relevant variables associated with diversity. Rather, it is intended to provide a point of departure for thinking about assessing the dimensions of learning related to appreciating diversity.

As it is imperative to identify variables early in the assessment process, this list provides the reader with several variables that might be used. As a general rule, the criterion (or dependent) variable essentially answers the question: What am I measuring? The predictor (or independent) variables, on the other hand, are those factors that are controlled or manipulated rather than observed. The predictor variable is often a grouping variable (for example, male versus female) and is the factor that is thought to be causal. For example, in most cases the dependent variable might be "appreciation of diversity" while "involvement in different interests and activities" may be one of the independent variables.

## D. Assessment Examples

Dr. Manny Peoples is the Assistant Director of Academic Affairs at Emerald Isle Community College. He is responsible for the Urban Scholars Program (USP). This program is designed to promote academic achievement and cocurricular involvement among high-achieving underrepresented students. To be eligible for the program, a student must be a member of a traditionally underrepresented group and maintain at least a 3.3 grade point average. The program consists of 15 weekly meetings organized around five units—scholarship, leadership, ethics, diversity, and social responsibility. To assess the effects of this program on students' level of appreciation for diversity, Dr. Peoples considered the following approaches:

Quantitative: At the beginning of the term, Dr. Peoples administered the *Diversity Awareness Profile* (Grote, 1995) and recorded each participant's initial score. During the unit on diversity, he is careful to address the issues and topics measured by the *Diversity Awareness Profile*. At the end of the term, Dr. Peoples administered the profile again and recorded each participant's score as a "post score." He calculated gain scores by subtracting the initial score from the post-score. This gave him a general idea of what participants gained from the Urban Scholars Program relative to diversity awareness and appreciation. In addition, students were required to maintain a log of their involvement in academic and extracurricular activities. This included the number of hours they spent working for student organizations, planning campus and community events, and participating in community service. Dr. Peoples analyzed the data by calculating correlations between the gain score and involvement hours.

Qualitative: Dr. Peoples used a case study approach to seek insight into the varying perspectives of diversity development of students participating in the program. Merriam (1998) described case study as an "intensive, holistic description and analysis of a single unit or bounded system" (p. 12). What distinguishes case study methodology from other qualitative approaches is the intensive focus on a "bounded system," which can be an individual, specific program, process, institution, or relationship (Jones, Torres, Arminio, 2006). Implicit in the selection of case study methodology is the assumption that there is something significant that can be learned from a single case (Stake, 2000). Believing that there was much to be gained in examining this single case, Dr. Peoples asked each participant to respond to the following: Before coming into the program, how would you have defined diversity? How would you define it now? How do you think you have changed as a result of this program? How would you have described yourself at the beginning of the program? How do you describe yourself now? He followed up with probes seeking specific examples and clarification of terms, events, and meanings. He also interviewed other stakeholders involved in the program. All interviews were tape recorded and sent to a professional for transcription. Dr. Peoples analyzed the resulting transcribed documents as well as observations of participants and documents related to the case, connecting differing student perspectives to corresponding stages in Bennett's Model of Intercultural Sensitivity.

## E. Available Instruments

A word of caution—be certain that these instruments yield the type of data that you need to examine your research topic or question. To do this, first determine what you want to know and then search for the instrument that will provide you with such information. Do not do the reverse. If none of these instruments yield the kind of data that you are interested in, you are advised to develop your own instrument to meet your needs.

*Diversity Awareness Profile (DAP)* by Karen Grote, 1995.
- 40-item instrument; designed to increase one's awareness of how s/he discriminates against, judge, or isolate others.
- Publisher: Jossey-Bass, 989 Market Street, San Francisco, CA 94103
- For more information: Conoley, J. C., & Impara, J. C. (Eds.). (1995).The twelfth mental measurements yearbook. Lincoln, NE: Buros Institute of Mental Measurements. www.unl.edu/buros

*Diversity Management Survey (DMS)* by Cresencio Torres, 2001.
- Used to determine how the structural aspects of an organization contribute to the management of diversity in the workplace.
- Publisher: Human Resource Development Press, 22 Amherst Road, Amherst, MA 01002-9709
- For more information: Plake, B. S., & Impara, J. C. (Eds.). (2001). The fourteenth mental measurements yearbook. Lincoln, NE: Buros Institute of Mental Measurements. www.unl.edu/buros

*Evaluating Diversity Training* by John M. Keller, Andrea Young, and Mary Riley, n.d.
- Designed to help diversity-training coordinators evaluate the effectiveness of training, instructors, and vendors.
- Publisher: Jossey-Bass, 989 Market Street, San Francisco, CA 94103
- For more information: www.unl.edu/buros

*Learning Environment Inventory* by B. J. Fraser, G. J. Anderson, H. J. Walberg, 1985.
- Designed to measure student perceptions of 15 dimensions of the social climate of classrooms.
- Publisher: Western Australia Institute of Technology
- For more information: Mitchell, J. V., Jr. (Ed.). (1985). The ninth mental measurements yearbook. Lincoln, NE: Buros Institute of Mental Measurements: www.unl.edu/buros

*Student Developmental Task and Lifestyle Assessment (SDTLA)*, Winston, Miller, and Cooper, 1999.
- Based on Chickering's Seven Vectors, the SDTLA measures college student developmental task achievement including (a) Establishing and Clarifying Purpose (52 items assessing career and lifestyle planning, cultural participation, and educational involvement); (b) Developing Autonomy (52 items measuring emotional, instrumental, and academic autonomy and interdependence); (c) Mature Interpersonal Relationships (42 items assessing tolerance, peer relationships, and salubrious life-style).
- Publisher: Student Development Associates, Inc.
- For more information: www.sdtla.appstate.edu/

Several purpose statements were adapted from those produced by the Buros Institute of Mental Measurements Test Reviews Online: www.unl.edu/buros

## F. Related Websites

| | |
|---|---|
| Diversity Web | www.diversityweb.org |
| Society for the Psychological Study of Social Issues | www.spssi.org |
| Fear of a Black America | www.fearofablackamerica.com |
| Diversity Reviews | www.diversityreviews.org |
| The Multicultural Advantage | www.multiculturaladvantage.com |
| Diversity Inc. | www.diversityinc.com |
| Diversity Initiative | www.diversityinitiative.org |
| Understanding Prejudice | www.understandingprejudice.org |

Diversity Working                    www.diversityworking.com

Diversity Database                   www.inform.umd.edu/EdRes/Topic/Diversity/

*Diversity Journal*                  www.diversityjournal.com

# G. References

Bean, J. P., & Eaton, S. B. (2000). A psychological model of college student retention. In J. M. Braxton (Ed.), *Reworking the student departure puzzle*, pp. 48-61. Nashville, TN: Vanderbilt University Press.

Bennett, M. J. (1986). A developmental approach to training for intercultural sensitivity. *International Journal of Intercultural Relations*, 10, 179-196.

Blimling, G. S. (2001). Diversity makes you smarter. *Journal of College Student Development*, 42(6), 517-519.

Bowen, W. G. & Bok, D. (1998). *The shape of the river*. Princeton, NJ. Princeton University Press.

Broido, E. M. (2000). The development of social justice allies during college: A phenomenological investigation, *Journal of College Student Development*, 41, 3-18.

Burd, S. (June 4, 2004). Colleges permit too many needy students to drop out, says report on graduation rates. *The Chronicle of Higher Education*, A19.

Brown University. (1986). *The American university and the pluralist ideal*. Providence, RI: Author.

Chickering, A. W. (1969). *Education and identity*. San Francisco: Jossey-Bass.

Chickering, A. W., & Reisser, L. (1993). *Education and identity* (2nd ed.). San Francisco: Jossey-Bass.

Commission on Minority Participation in Education and American Life (1988). *One-third of a nation*. Author.

Cross, W. E., Jr. (1971). Toward a psychology of black liberation: The negro-to-black conversion experience. *Black World*, 20(9), 13-27.

Cross, W. E., Jr. (1978). The Thomas and Cross models of psychological Nigrescence: A review. *Journal of Black Psychology*, 5, 13-31.

D'Augelli, A. R. (1991). Gay men in college: Identity processes and adaptations. *Journal of College Student Development*, 32, 140-146.

Evans, N. J., Forney, D. S., & Guido-Brito, F. (1998). *Student development in college: Theory, research, and practice*. San Francisco: Jossey-Bass.

Green, M. F. (Ed.). (1989). *Minorities on campus: A handbook for enhancing diversity*. Washington, DC: American Council on Education.

Helms, J. E. (1995). An update of Helms's White and People of Color racial idenity models. In J. G. Ponterotto, J. M. Casias, L. A. Suzuki, & C. M. Alexander (Eds.), *Handbook of multicultural counseling* (pp. 181-198). Thousand Oaks, CA: Sage.

Jones, S. R., Torres, V., & Arminio, J. (2006). *Negotiating the complexities of qualitative research*. New York: Brunner-Routledge.

Kitchener, K. S., & King, P. M. (1981). Reflective judgment: Concepts of justification and their relationship to age and education. *Journal of Applied Developmental Psychology*, 2, 89-116.

Merriam, S. B. (1998). *Qualitative research and case study applications in education*. San Francisco: Jossey-Bass.

Pedersen, P. (1988). *Handbook for developing multicultural awareness*. Alexandria, VA: American Association of Counseling and Development.

Perry, W. G., Jr. (1968). *Forms of intellectual and ethical development in the college years: A scheme*. New York: Holt, Rinehart, & Winston.

Perry, W. G., Jr. (1978). Sharing in the cost of growth. In C. A. Parker (Ed.), *Encouraging development in college students* (pp. 267-273). Minneapolis: University of Minnesota Press.

Perry, W. G., Jr. (1981). Cognitive and ethical growth: The making of meaning. In A. W. Chickering & Associates (Eds.), *The modern American college: Responding to the new realities of diverse students and a changing society* (pp. 76-116). San Francisco: Jossey-Bass.

Phinney, J. S. (1989). Stages of ethnic identity development in minority.

Piaget, J. (1950). *The psychology of intelligence* (M. Piercy & D. E. Berlyne, Trans.). London: Routledge & Kegan Paul.

Piaget, J. (1952). *The origins of intelligence in children*. New York: International Universities Press.

Reason, R. D., Roosa Millar, E. A., & Scales, T. C. (2005). Toward a model of racial justice ally development. *Journal of College Student Development*, 46(5), 530-546.

Sedlacek, W. E. (2004). *Beyond the big test: Non-cognitive assessment in higher education*. San Francisco: Jossey-Bass.

Schmidt, P. (June 3, 2003). Why not a remedy for past discrimination. *The Chronicle of Higher Education*, A20.

Stake, R. E. (2000). Case studies. In N. K. Denzin & Y. S. Lincoln (Eds.) *Handbook of qualitative research* (2nd ed, pp. 435-454). Thousand Oaks, CA: Sage.

Talbot, D. M. (2003). Multiculturalism (pp. 423-446). In S. R. Komives & D. B. Woodward (Eds.), *Student Services: A handbook for the profession*. San Francisco: Jossey-Bass.

Torres, V. (1996). *Empirical studies in Latino/Latina ethnic identity*. Paper presented at the National Association of Student Personnel Administrators National Conference, Baltimore, MD.

## H. Recommended Reading

Adams, M., Blumenfeld, N. J., Caseneda, R., Hackman, H. W., Peters, M. L., Zuniga, X. (2000). *Readings for diversity and social justice*. New York: Falmer Press.

Banks, J. (2005). *Cultural diversity and education: Foundations, curriculum, and teaching* (5th ed.). New York: Allyn & Bacon.

Cafferty, S. J., & Chestang, L. (Eds.). (1976). *The diverse society: Implications for social policy*. Washington, DC: NASW Press.

Cross, W. E., Jr. (1971). Toward a psychology of black liberation: The negro-to-black conversion experience. *Black World*, 20(9), 13-27.

Cross, W. E., Jr. (1978). The Thomas and Cross models of psychological Nigrescence: A review. *Journal of Black Psychology*, 5, 13-31.

D'Augelli, A. R. (1991). Gay men in college: Identity processes and adaptations. *Journal of College Student Development*, 32, 140-146.

Hunter, S., & Hickerson, J. C. (2003). *Affirmative practice: Understanding and working with Lesbian, Gay, Bisexual, and Transgender Persons*. Washington, DC: NASW Press.

Martin, E. P., & Martin, J. M. (2003). *Spirituality and the Black helping tradition in social work*. Washington, DC: NASW Press.

Momsen, J., & Kinnaird, V. (1993). *Different places, different voices*. New York: Routledge.

Orfield, G., & Kurlaender, M. (2001). *Diversity challenged: Evidence on the impact of affirmative action*. Cambridge, MA: Harvard Education Publishing Group.

Wijeyesinghe, C. L. & Jackson, B.W., III, (Eds). (2001). *New perspectives on racial identity development*. New York: New York University Press.

# Personal and Educational Goals

## A. Introduction

It was suggested by Pascarella and Terenzini (2005) that studies on change during college were less far-reaching in the 1990s literature than in the body of literature that appeared prior to the 1990s. Their most recent work uncovered little evidence to counter the conclusion made in their earlier meta analysis that students make significant gains in knowledge and become more "critical, reflective, and sophisticated thinkers" during college (p. 573). Using such cognitive abilities, college students are able to evaluate themselves better and are more capable of setting reasonable expectations and goals.

In his book, *When Dreams and Heroes Died*, Arthur Levine (1980), then senior fellow at The Carnegie Foundation for the Advancement of Teaching, described a college generation that was both idealistic and pragmatic, liberal and conservative, optimistic and pessimistic. These terms appeared confusingly contradictory at first until Levine pointed out that they refer to different things. For example, students of the college generation of the 1970s were optimistic about their own future while being pessimistic about the future of the country. Such distinctions were helpful for understanding that generation and their preference for setting moderate, proximate personal goals rather than long-term or collective goals.

Levine's seminal work is confirmed by recent research on the current college generation called *The Millenials* (Howe & Strauss, 2000). In their book, *Millenials Rising*, the authors described a new generation that is qualitatively different from preceding cohorts. Reversing the negative trend towards rule breaking and pessimism, today's college generation tends to accept authority, cooperate on teams, follow the rules, and believe in themselves and the future of the nation.

This optimism coupled with high levels of achievement yield a college generation charged with a certain rapidity combined with high expectations, and goals. In fact, Howe and Strauss reported that three students in five believe that they can be President of the United States someday. A larger majority describe themselves as cutting edge and believe that they can change the world.

An important question to consider is: what is the function of college for such high thinking, optimistic youths? Burton Clark (1960) once argued that higher education serves a "cooling out" function for students with unrealistic educational ambitions and goals. For example, a student who aspires to be a nurse despite a poor record of academic performance might be encouraged to study as a nurse's assistant or be advised to reassess such a goal in light of exhibited lack of qualifications and preparation.

Setting realistic educational and personal goals is one of the 16 learning and development outcome domains identified by the Council for the Advancement of Standards in Higher Education. Indicators of its achievement include setting individual goals and articulating one's goals and objectives. CAS strongly encourages all student affairs professionals and educators to consider how their programs and services impact student learning and achievement of such outcomes.

## B. Theoretical Contexts for Learning and Development

Student development theory provides a guide for understanding growth and change in young adults. In fact, such theory has proved useful in examining what happens to students during the college years. It also provides student affairs practitioners with information that can be used to create interventions designed to enhance student learning and development (Evans, Forney, & Guido-Brito, 1998). Developmental theory yields information about factors contributing to development in cognitive, affective, and behavioral domains such as those discussed in this text.

While there seems to be no clear theory on educational and personal goals per se, there are a number of theories that relate to this domain. To the extent that setting educational and personal goals is related to identity, realistic self-appraisal, and self-efficacy the works of Perry, Chickering, and Loevinger are important to this theoretical discussion. Perry (1968) set forth a theory consisting of nine positions. His scheme characterized a movement from a basic duality way of thinking to increasingly complex ways of viewing the world. This may mirror the shift away from either achieving or not achieving one's goals towards a more complex and well-reasoned assessment of one's goals. For example, those who think more complexly are able to see the many shades of gray related to achieving goals (e.g., achieving goals, achieving parts of a goal, re-evaluating the appropriateness of goals).

Chickering's (1969) seven vectors were proposed to describe the formation of identity (see also Chickering & Reisser, 1993). He argued that the process of development consisted of seven vectors including developing competence, managing emotions, moving through autonomy toward interdependence, developing mature relationships, establishing identity, developing purpose, and developing integrity. The developing purpose vector consists of establishing "clear vocational goals and making meaningful commitments to specific personal interests and activities" (Evans, Forney, & Guido-Brito, 1998, p. 40). He also suggested that lifestyle and family factors influence goal setting and decision-making. His work is important for understanding learning and development in this domain.

Finally, Loevinger (1976) articulated an explanation of ego development as progressions along a continuum. Her theory focused on transition from one stage to the next. Ego development is best summarized as a process of restructuring one's personality from self-protection and opportunism to a more integrated frame of reference. This may be related to the restructuring that is necessary to reposition one's personal and educational goals. That is, as an individuals' ego develops their perspective changes and may allow (if not require) them to revisit and/or reevaluate goals set previously.

There is a need for additional research in this area given the number of different arenas in which it is observed. Too, additional knowledge is needed to understand the relationship between educational and personal goals and other domains such as intellectual development, self-appraisal, and self-esteem. Despite these areas of need, the current literature provides a basis for relevant theoretical discussion. It should also be noted that the Cooperative Institutional Research Program (CIRP) provides data on students' goals and may be useful to those interested in students' perspectives of their goals upon entering the instituion.

## C. Relevant variables

- sets and articulates individual goals
- identifies personal goals and objectives
- sets realistic goals
- understands the effect of one's goals on self
- exhibits behaviors consistent with one's goals
- sets and articulates educational goals
- identifies educational goals and objectives
- uses goals to make decisions
- understands the effect of one's goals on others
- identifies obstacles to achieving goals and ways to overcome them

This list of variables is by no means an exhaustive list of all of the relevant variables associated with personal and educational goals. Rather, it is intended to provide a point of departure for thinking about assessing the dimensions of learning related to personal and educational goals.

As it is imperative to identify variables early in the assessment process, this list provides the reader with several variables that might be used. As a general rule, the criterion (or dependent) variable essentially answers the question: What am I measuring? The predictor (or independent) variables, on the other hand, are those factors that are controlled or manipulated rather than observed. The predictor variable is often a grouping variable (for example, gender or year in college) and is the factor that is thought to be causal. For example, in most cases the dependent variable is the learning outcome while "uses goals to make decisions" may be one of the independent variables.

## D. Assessment Examples

Dr. Aimee High is the Vice Provost for Academic Affairs at The University of Hamilton. The university is located in the rural region of a southeastern state. The institution enrolls more than 20,000 undergraduate students with a first- year class of approximately 4,500. Recent institutional reports suggest that the number of first-year students who fail to advance to their second-year in college has increased dramatically over the past 10 years. The President and Board of Visitors adopt retention as an institutional priority and rally for the support of campus administrators, faculty members, and staff persons. Dr. High embraces the institutional goal and shares the President's vision with her staff. To do this, she presents startling facts during the next Academic Affairs division-wide meeting. Through a combination of text, graphs, and tables, she points out that undergraduate retention has decreased steadily over the past 10 years with less than 50% of all first-year students persisting to the second-year of college. In her concluding slides, she summarizes recent national findings about the factors that influence retention and attrition in college.

Dr. High emphasizes the fact that retention/attrition is a function of the interaction between the person and his or her college environment. This is what Tinto (1975) refered to as the academic and social integration of students into the college experience. Dr. High also pointed out that both the student and the institution play a role in the retention/departure puzzle. Students come to college with a number of expectations and goals in mind. The institution (administrators, faculty, staff) also has expectations of its students that must be met if both student and institution are to be deemed successful. The degree to which both sets of expectations are met is directly proportional to the students' level of success in college.

With this in mind, Dr. High announces that the division will conduct a comprehensive assessment to explore these factors. Specifically, Dr. High and her team will investigate the expectations and goals of college students prior to their first year and examine the influence of both personal and institutional expectations on persistence in college. They consider the following approaches:

1. Quantitative: To examine this issue, Dr. High advises her team to use pre-existing data that has been collected and is available to university senior administrators and faculty members. Dr. Lenna Hand is the Director of Assessment at The University of Hamilton and she agrees to provide Dr. High with two years of data collected through the *College Student Expectations Questionnaire (CSXQ)* and the *College Student Experiences Questionnaire (CSEQ)*. The CSXQ is adapted from the CSEQ and was designed to assess new students' motivations and goals. The CSXQ was administered to all accepted first- year students prior to the start of their first semester. It yields information about new students' expectations regarding how and with whom they will spend their time in college. The researchers record CSXQ scores as a pre-test measure representing new students' expectations and goals. The CSEQ was administered to the same group of students at the end of their first-year or before a student departed from the University during the first year. The CSEQ represents a post-test score and allows the team to assess the degree to which student and institutional expectations are met. In addition, all students in the database were coded as "persisters" (=1) and "non-persisters" (=0). Persisters were those students who completed their first year and enrolled for their second year of college. Non-persisters either failed to complete their first year of college or completed their first year but failed to enroll in the second-year. This dichotomous factor was used as the dependent variable in a regression analyses.

   To describe the expectations of new students, descriptive statistics were used to summarize the results of the CSXQ data. To measure the influence of student and institutional expectations/goals on persistence in college, logistic regression techniques were used to test the ability of prior expectations (as measured by the CSXQ) and student-institutional characteristics like interactions, goals, and expectations (as measured by the CSEQ) to predict the probability of persisting in college from freshman to sophomore year.

2. Qualitative: To assess the contribution of college experiences on students' personal and educational goals, the team uses a case study approach to gather information. While a quantitative researcher tends to gather data on a large number of cases, a qualitative researcher may "use a case study approach, in which she gathers a large amount of information on one or a few cases, goes into greater depth, and gets more detail on the cases that she examines" (Neuman, 1994, p. 321). "The case study is a frequently used approach to gathering qualitative information about a program" (Worthen, Sanders, & Fitzpatrick, 1997, p. 373). This is particularly useful in assessment and evaluation when the goal is to provide in-depth information about a single program rather than to generalize to "all programs" or a broader population (Guba & Lincoln, 1981; Stake, 1994).

   To this end, the researchers collect a wealth of information on 10 first-year students assuming that 1 out of 2, on average, will fail to persist. Participants were asked to record their personal and educational goals prior to beginning their first semester in college. Over the next year, researchers gathered information about each respondent's extracurricular involvement, courses taken, academic major, college experiences, employment and work-study, and financial aid awards. In addition, The University of Hamilton requires all entering students to take a first-year seminar. In this course, students are expected to maintain an on-going journal cataloging their experiences during the first-year in college and reflecting on how their goals and expectations changed throughout the year. The 10 students selected for the in-depth case study were asked to submit their first-year seminar journals to the research team for evaluation periodically. Drawing on information from a variety of sources, the researchers became "immersed" (Neuman, 1994, p. 321) in the data and searched for patterns in the lives, actions, words, and experiences of these students. The rich, thick data allowed the researchers to paint a vivid in-depth image of the influence of college on setting, reappraising, and possibly attaining personal and educational goals.

## E. Available Instruments

A word of caution—be certain that these instruments yield the type of data that you need to assess learning and development in this domain. To do this, first determine what you want to know and then search for the instrument that will provide you with such information. Do not do the reverse. If none of these instruments yield the kind of data that you are interested in, you are advised to develop your own instrument to meet your specific needs.

*Student Goals Exploration* by Joan S. Stark, Malcom A. Lowther, Kathleen M. Shaw, and Paula L. Sossen, 1998.
- Used to assist researchers to better understand the academic goals of college students.
- Publisher: National Center for Research to Improve Postsecondary Teaching and Learning, 2400 School of Education Building, The University of Michigan, Ann Arbor, MI 48109-1259.
- For more information: Impara, J. C., & Plake, B. S. (Eds.). (1998). The thirteenth mental measurements yearbook. Lincoln, NE: Buros Institute of Mental Measurements. www.unl.edu/buros

*Assessment of Core Goals (ACG)* by C. W. Nicols, n.d.
- Designed to identify core goals and to identify activities that will lead to achievement of these goals.
- Publisher: Mind Garden, Inc., 1690 Woodside Road, Suite 202, Redwood City, CA 94061, 650-261-3500, info@mindgarden.com.
- For more information: www.mindgarden.com.

*Career Beliefs Inventory (CBI)* by John D. Krumboltz, n.d.
- Constructed to assist people in identifying career beliefs that may influence career goals.
- Publisher: CPP, Inc., 3803 East Bayshore Road, Palo Alto, CA 94303, 800-624-1765, knw@cpp-dc.com.
- For more information: www.cpp-db.com

*Community College Goals Inventory (CCGI)* by ETS Community and Junior College Programs, n.d.
- Designed to help community college students identify their goals and establish priorities.
- Publisher: Educational Testing Service, Publication Order Services, PO Box 6736, Princeton, NJ 08541-6736, 609-921-9000, etsinfo@ets.org.
- For more information: www.ets.org

*College Student Expectations Questionnaire (CSXQ)* by George D. Kuh and Robert C. Pace, 1998.
- Designed to evaluate student's expectations for college including their motivations, future plans, and goals.
- Publisher: Indiana University Center for Postsecondary Research and Planning, 1913 East 7th Street, Ashton-Aley Hall, Suite 102, Bloomington, IN 47405-7510, nsse@indiana.edu.
- For more information: www.iub.edu/~cseq

Several purpose statements were adapted from those produced by the Buros Institute of Mental Measurements Test Reviews Online: www.unl.edu/buros

## F. Related Websites

Personal Goal Setting          www.mindtools.com

Goal Setting Guide             www.goal-setting-guide.com

Goal Setting                   www.topachievement.com/goalsetting.html

Goals for Everyone             www.mygoals.com

Time Management and Goals      www.time-management-guide.com

## G. References

Chickering, A. W. (1969). *Education and identity*. San Francisco: Jossey-Bass.

Chickering, A. W., & Reisser, L. (1993). *Education and identity* (2nd ed.). San Francisco: Jossey-Bass.

Clark, B. R. (1960). The cooling out function in higher education. *The American Journal of Sociology*, 65, 569-576.

Evans, N. J., Forney, D. S., & Guido-Brito, F. (1998). Student development in college: Theory, research, and practice. San Francisco: Jossey-Bass.

Guba, E. G., & Lincoln, Y. S. (1981). *Effective evaluation*. San Francisco: Jossey-Bass.

Howe, N., & Strauss, W. (2000). *Millenials Rising: The next great generation*. New York: Vintage Books.

Loevinger, J. (1976). *Ego development: Conceptions and theories*. San Francisco: Jossey-Bass.

Levine, A. (1980). *When dreams and heroes died: A portrait of today's college student*. San Francisco: Jossey-Bass.

Neuman, W. L. (1994). *Social research methods: Qualitative and quantitative approaches* (2nd ed.). Needham Heights, MA: Allyn and Bacon.

Pascarella, E. T., & Terenzini, P. T. (2005). *How college affects students: A third decade of research*. San Francisco: Jossey-Bass.

Perry, W. G., Jr. (1968). F*orms of intellectual and ethical development in the college years: A scheme*. New York: Holt, Rinehart & Winston.

Stake, R. E. (1994). Case studies. In N. K. Denzin & Y. S. Lincoln (Eds.), *Handbook of qualitative research*. Thousand Oaks, CA: Sage.

Tinto, V. (1975). Dropout from higher education: A theoretical synthesis of recent research. *Review of Educational Research*, 45(1), 89-125.

Worthen, B. R., Sanders, J. R., & Fitzpatrick, J. L. (1997). *Program evaluation: Alternative approaches and practical guidelines* (2nd ed.). White Plains, NY: Longman.

## H. Recommended Reading

Ellis, K. (1998). *The magic lamp: Goal setting for people who hate setting goals.* New York Three Rivers Press.

Fossland, C. (2005). *Ten reasons to have an inspired, world changing goal.* Retrieved June 8, 2005, from http://ezinearticles.com/?Ten-Reasons-To-Have-an-Inspired,-World-Changing-Goal&id=41864

St. Laurent, J. (2005). *How to achieve any goal, now!* Retrieved June 8, 2005, from http://ezinearticles.com/?How-To-Achieve-Any-Goal,-NOW!&id=41041

# Healthy Behavior

Guest Authors: Dr. Patricia Fabiano, Dr. Richard Keeling, and Dr. Pam Viele

## A. Introduction

Health is best understood as capacity – the presence of conditions that enable individuals and communities to work, learn, participate as citizens, and have strong human relationships. Health, in other words, embraces many elements of life; it is not simply the absence of disease or injury, and it is not just a medical, or clinical, quality. Among students in higher education, health supports the capacity to learn; when health is compromised, learning is constrained. Health problems among students include the universe of personal, developmental, social, physical, and mental issues that reduce their capacity to learn – from disruptions in relationships or stress to chronic intrapersonal, physical or psychological illnesses.

The most pressing health problems affecting most students' lives are health risk behaviors and psychological concerns. A significant minority of undergraduates – especially, undergraduates of traditional age – experience serious physical illnesses that limit their ability to learn and participate in campus life; students who have diabetes or asthma are far more common examples than their rare peers with cancer or HIV/AIDS. In extreme cases, severe illnesses or injuries may interrupt studies or postpone graduation. But for most students, physical illnesses experienced during college are minor and episodic; their impact on learning is brief and moderate.

Far more frequently, students' learning is restrained by psychosocial and psychological concerns (especially stress, depression, bipolar disorder, and attention deficit hyperactivity disorder), relationship issues (such as distraction because of the illness or struggles of a friend or family member), and the presence or consequences of health risk behaviors (including alcohol, tobacco, and other drug abuse; unprotected sexual activity; accidental injuries; and violence). Compelling data from the Centers for Disease Control and Prevention's National College Health Risk Behavior Survey (NCHRBS) and American College Health Association's National College Health Assessment (NCHA) reveal that intrapersonal, psychological, and relationship concerns are the primary problems identified by students as causes of interference with academic achievement.

The unique features of the campus environment, social networks among students, and dynamic developmental characteristics of youth give special emphasis to the role of communities in influencing the health of their members. Students consciously and unconsciously make decisions that affect their health – and the health of others – in the context of the values, traditions, and customs of the campus; health-related norms and preferences among their peers; social and cultural values about health and its determinants and importance; and the images and valences of health and health behaviors in entertainment and advertising media. The effect of college on the drinking behavior of entering first-year students is well documented, as one example; matriculation is associated with immediate increases in the proportion of students who drink, drink heavily, and experience negative consequences of their drinking.

The health effects of college vary, of course, depending on institutional characteristics, student demographics, and region. But it is not possible to address the health behaviors, health status, or health concerns of students as individuals in isolation from their roles and place in campus communities. To reduce the harm done by abusive drinking on campus, for example, it is necessary to change the drinking patterns of the student population – which means changing campus culture itself. For example, students who abstain from alcohol use are also frequently affected by those students who do use alcohol. Interrupted sleep, study, and decreased quality of social relationships create a dysfunctional social environment that impedes student learning.

Colleges and universities that wish to enhance student learning and support academic achievement—including persistence, retention, and graduation—will inevitably and properly attend to the health of students—both as individuals and as members of various campus and off-campus communities that have their own health characteristics. Attention to the health of students will reasonably include, in most circumstances, all of these elements:

- Prevention, health promotion, and wellness programs to improve campus patterns of health enhancing or health risk behaviors, values, and attitudes
- Outreach, surveillance, and screening or case-finding services to identify students who need mental health or health behavior interventions
- Interventions to support healthier and safer patterns of personal health risk behavior
- Public health surveillance and interventions
- Comprehensive psychological services, including counseling, psychiatric services, consultation, and crisis response
- Basic ambulatory primary care medical and nursing services, including women's health care—which should be provided in a developmental and educational context; clinical services that are not customized for students' specific needs and the context of academic and campus culture do not meet the needs of colleges and universities.

Responsibility for advancing the health of students should be understood broadly; it is shared by health educators, health care providers, professional counselors, nutritionists and dietitians, athletic trainers, residence life staff, and members of the faculty. The settings in which health can productively be addressed on campus are multiple – classrooms, community service programs, residence halls, recreation centers, dining halls, libraries, performance spaces, and green space, in addition to health clinics and counseling centers. Providing clinical care in a traditional college health center is not alone a sufficient response to the health needs of students in any setting.

## B. Theoretical Contexts for Learning and Development

Many useful models and theories describe and predict human behavior. The interplay of youth development, student development, psychosocial development, and health behavior change theories provides a rich palette from which to paint a picture that illustrates the complexity of college student health behaviors. It is imperative that those who seek to understand the interrelationships of college students, college environments, and college resources—including how those interrelationships result in health-related decision-making—consider the theoretical constructs that explain and predict health behaviors (Underhile, 2000). The figure below presents a brief, albeit incomplete, example of four key theoretical constructs useful to higher education professionals.

**Theory:** Theory of Moral Development

**Author:** Kohlberg, L. (1971)

**Major constructs:** Moral reasoning occurs through a three-level sequence, with each level consisting of two stages. These levels (Preconventional, Conventional, and Principled) allow individuals to move from an egocentric and concrete worldview through interpersonal and social systems of morality and arrive at universal morality and broad conceptual ethics.

**Application to college health:** Students develop important personal and social skills that progressively increase their ability to consider how personal behaviors contribute to or impede their quality of life and that of their peers. Universal skills (like those described by Fetro & Drolet, 2000) include the ability to make thoughtful decisions, choose healthy stress management strategies, clearly communicate personal values and boundaries, and set and adhere to important personal goals.

**Theory:** Psychosocial Theory of Student Development

**Author:** Chickering, A.W. (1969)

**Major constructs:** Development during late adolescence and early adulthood could be characterized as seven major areas or vectors of development: competence, emotions, autonomy, identity, interpersonal relationships, purpose, and integrity.

**Application to college health:** These vectors include description of achievement of important health-related skills such as, mastery of reflective skills to manage impulses, development of a sense of independence, ability to recognize experiences that are safe or self-destructive, management of emotions, tolerance of others, ability to envision a preferred future, and development of congruence between personal values and expression of those values in one's behaviors.

**Theory:** Social Cognitive Theory

**Author:** Bandura, A. (1977).

**Major Constructs:** Social cognitive theory (SCT) provides a framework through which individual and group behavior may be understood and predicted; methods for influencing behavior can be identified; and interventions for health-related risk behaviors may be developed. Reciprocal determinism, symbolizing capability, vicarious capability, forethought capability, self-regulatory capability, and self-reflective capability are key constructs to SCT.

**Application to College Health:** SCT has been especially useful as a lens through which to consider the development of societal standards and values. Health behaviors—those that increase the likelihood of negative consequences and those that decrease the likelihood of negative consequences—are often behavioral expressions of students' perception of peer norms. SCT provides a useful tool for understanding and predicting, and influencing students' health-related behaviors.

**Theory:** Ecological Perspective

**Author:** McLeroy, K. R., Bibeau, D. Steckler, A., Glanz, K. (1988)

**Major Constructs:** The ecological perspective illustrates the synergistic relationship between and among individuals, physical environments, and socio-cultural environments. Two major constructs elucidate the ecological perspective: 1) multiple levels of influence and 2) reciprocal causation. Multiple levels of influence include five levels of health behaviors and the contexts in which they occur: 1) intrapersonal factors; 2) interpersonal factors; 3) institutional factors; 4) community factors; and 5) public policy factors. Reciprocal causation describes the interrelationship and influence power between individuals and their peers.

**Application to College Health:** The ecological perspective is useful in considering the role of institutions of higher education as complex organizations that through policy and practice comprise physical and social environments. Further, the ecological perspective illuminates how students' health-related behaviors are impacted by the organizational culture of the institution.

## C. Relevant Variables

These variables emphasize that assessments of health status are closely linked to assessments of learning, social functioning, and participation in community. For example, it is established in the literature that sleep patterns or the quality of breakfast nutrition are strong determinants of capacity to learn among youth; research or assessment projects in college might address a palette of behavioral, social, and environmental determinants of the ability to learn. Qualities that might be assessed in determining the health status of students include:

- Is able to learn at the level of their potential
- Demonstrates and reports engagement with academic and co-curricular activities and challenges in college
- Chooses and exhibits behaviors that promote health, reduce risk, and strengthen relationships
- Participates in recreation and fitness activities
- Demonstrates positive self-care, including healthy diet, regular exercise, personal hygiene, and sufficient sleep in routine patterns
- Demonstrates emotional well-being and care-taking in relation to self and others
- Understands and can explain the relationship between health and one's capacity to meet personal, academic, and long-term goals
- Exhibits caring attitudes and forms authentic and mutually rewarding human relationships
- Appreciates and responds to the opportunities and challenges of human differences; can affirm differences of opinion and world-view
- Understands the essential connections between personal health and the quality of the natural, campus, and human environments; can articulate how the health of individuals is linked to the health of the natural environment and of their community
- Recognizes their role in fostering and sustaining a sense of community

These variables (and others) of healthy students living in healthy communities and environments can form the basis for assessment activities.

## D. Assessment Examples

### Background on the Interest in "Student Health"

The construction and dedication of the new state-of-the-art Recreation Center at Central State University (CSU), a four-year comprehensive public institution in the Midwest with an enrollment of 13,000 undergraduate and 3,500 graduate students, stimulated a campus-wide conversation about the "health habits" of CSU students. At a recent meeting of the President's Council, composed of Deans, Directors, and University Vice Presidents, the new Director of the Recreation Center reported that, during the Center's first nine months of operation, electronic student ID card readers recorded over 8,000 visits per month. She was quick to point out, however, that over half of these 8,000 visits were repeat users. She told the President's Council that a key unanswered question was: "Which students among CSU's 16,500 students were not using the Recreation Center and why?"

The Recreation Center Director's candid report added to the larger question puzzling members of the President's Council: "How is the health status of CSU students impacting learning?" Two academic deans spoke up about what they had heard a recent Faculty Senate forum. Several distraught faculty members had stated that they did not know how—nor did they want to know how—to address the stress and anxiety levels among students in their classes. University Counsel described recent cases in the news where Universities had been charged by parents as "negligent" in the care of their children with mental health problems. The Vice President for External Affairs added that neighbors whose properties were contiguous to campus complained bitterly about the alcohol-fueled "loud and disruptive" parties that seemed to be escalating. Finally, the Vice President for Student Affairs said that health data on graduating high-school seniors from the state's public school system suggested that new students who would be entering CSU in the fall had a higher incidence of depression, increased alcohol and other drug use, and less exercise per week than all previous cohorts of high-school seniors.

### Student Health Status Task Force

Given the level of concern and the variety of troublesome indicators describing the possible health status of CSU students, the President asked the Vice President of Student Affairs to convene a Task Force to study the health of students and to make recommendations to the President's Council on their findings.

The Vice President of Student Affairs assembled the members of the CSU community to participate in the Student Health Status Task Force.

He asked each member to collect relevant data from their unit that would shed light on the issue of the overall "health status" of CSU students and to present that data to educate the Task Force:

At a subsequent meeting at which the data was presented and discussed, the Health Promotion and Wellness Services Director pointed out that the data, with the exception of the utilization summaries from the Recreation Center, provided a perspective on the "problems" and "illnesses" of CSU students. She suggested that the data, in fact, were not indicators of "health status;" rather, they were better understood as clinical indicators of "illness status." She urged the group to think about a broader definition of health that included the "individual health behaviors" *and* larger environmental factors on campus and in the community that influence the health of all CSU students. She stated that several key professional organizations such as National Association of Student Personnel Administrators (NASPA), American College Personnel Association (ACPA), the American College Health Association (ACHS), National Intramural-Recreational Sports Associations (NIRSA), and others were advocating that *all professionals* on college campuses attend to the health of students because "health" was a critical correlate of learning.

### A Plan to Understand Student Health & Its Relationship to Learning Outcomes

Members of the Task Force felt a shift take place in their thinking. While it had been important to understand all the "illness" data that characterized "some" of their students, they understood that this data was, by definition, limited by the relatively small number of students who used a particular service or program. It became equally important to the Task Force to undertake an assessment plan that would address variables affecting the "health" of "most" of their students, with specific attention given to the effects of health on learning. The following assessment options were generated to report to the Vice President for Student Affairs as necessary prerequisites to understand the health status of CSW students:

1. Conduct a population-based assessment of student health status, needs, and assets. The National College Health Assessment (ACHA, 2002) was recommended because it provides (a) standardized measures with

published reliability and validity data, (b) a national comparison group of nearly a quarter million college students, and (c) data from questions that inquire into the connection between health status and academic progress.

2. Conduct a population-based assessment of current student alcohol and drug use, consequences, and perceptions using a valid and reliable nationally standardized instrument such as the National College Health Assessment's alcohol and drug scales, the Core Institute's Survey of Alcohol and Other Drug Use, or the Harvard College Alcohol Survey.

3. Conduct an environmental assessment of social, cultural, economic, and/or political factors that may contribute to or compromise the health of students and adversely impact learning and academic success. Consult published sources on campus environmental assessments such as the Campus Alcohol Risk Assessment Guide published by the Higher Education Center for Alcohol and Other Drug Prevention (available at http://www.edc.org/hec/pubs/cara.pdf).

4. Design, implement, and analyze the results of a series of systematic qualitative, in-depth group interviews (focus groups) with randomly selected CSU students stratified by gender-identity, year in school, and on- or off-campus residential status. The purpose of the assessment is to understand how students construct the meaning of "health" and how they describe the individual and community level factors that support and/or hinder their health and the academic impacts of these health impediments.

5. Conduct interviews with key faculty members (identified by the Faculty Senate) to understand the challenges to students' health status, with an emphasis on emotional health, present to faculty in the classroom. In addition to discerning the problems faculty face, faculty also will be queried for their suggestions for strategies to assist both them and their students.

6. Include the Coordinator of the Ethnic Student Center as a member of the Task Force and collaborate with him or her and staff to identify and understand the specific cultural, social, economic, and other factors that influence the health and well-being of the CSU's largest minority groups: Native American and first-generation East Asian immigrant students. Work with the Coordinator and student leaders to design culturally competent assessment processes.

7. Convene a Presidential-level meeting of key Neighborhood Association and campus community members, including student leaders and students who live off-campus, to begin a conversation about "common ground" for improving the health and safety of all—long-term residents and students—who live in the neighborhoods adjacent to the campus.

Once the data from all these sources were analyzed and collated to form a comprehensive assessment of the current status of "health" and its impacts on learning among CSU students, the Task Force suggested to the President that they would then be ready to develop meaningful, manageable, and measurable goals and objectives to advance the health of students and the campus community.

## E. Available Instruments

A word of caution—be certain that these instruments yield the type of data that you need to assess your program's effectiveness. To do this, first determine what you want to know and then search for the appropriate recourses. Do not do the reverse. The data that you seek is not Available, then develop your own instrument to meet your specific needs.

1. American College Health Association-National College Health Assessment (ACHA, 2005) http://www.acha-ncha.org/

2. Core Institute's Survey of Alcohol and Other Drug Use (nd) http://www.coresurvey.com/

3. Campus Alcohol Risk Assessment Guide published by the Higher Education Center for Alcohol and Other Drug Prevention (nd) http://www.edc.org/hec/pubs/cara.pdf

4. Schuh and Upcraft's (2001) Assessment Practice in Student Affairs: An Application Manual (Chapter 12: Environmental Assessment).

5. Hays, R. D., Sherbourne, C. D., & Mazel, R. (1995). Medical outcomes study core measures of health-related quality of life. http://www.rand.org/pubs/monograph_reports/MR162/index/

6. Higher Education Research Institute – http://www.gseis.ucla.edu/heri/heri.html

    The Cooperative Institutional Research Program (CIRP) is a national longitudinal study of the American higher education system. Established in 1966 at the American Council on Education, the CIRP is now administered by the Higher Education Research Institute under the direction of John H. Pryor. The CIRP is the nation's largest and oldest empirical study of higher education, involving data on some 1,800 institutions and over 11 million students. It is regarded as the most comprehensive source of information on college students. The annual report of the CIRP Freshman Survey provides normative data on each year's entering college students. http://www.gseis.ucla.edu/heri/cirp.html

    Your First College Year (YFCY) is the only national survey designed specifically to assess the academic and personal development of students over the first year of college. Developed through a collaboration between HERI and the Policy Center on the First Year of College at Brevard College, YFCY enables institutions to identify features of the first year that encourage student learning, involvement, satisfaction, retention and success, thereby enhancing first-year programs and retention strategies at campuses across the country. http://www.gseis.ucla.edu/heri/yfcy/

    College Student Survey: The Survey Instrument is typically administered to senior students or used as an "exit" survey. It covers a broad range of outcomes including: academic achievement and engagement; satisfaction with the college experience; student involvement; cognitive and affective development; student values, attitudes, and goals; degree aspirations and career plans; Internet and other technology use. The CSS can be used as a "stand-alone" instrument or to follow-up another CIRP Survey. The CSS post-test contains many items on the CIRP Freshman Survey and the YFCY Survey. The CSS also includes space for up to 30 institution specific questions. http://www.gseis.ucla.edu/heri/css.html

7. *Salubrious Lifestyle Scale from the Student Developmental Task and Lifestyle Assessment (SDTLA)* by Winston, Miller, & Cooper (1997). Measures via self-report the degree to which students exhibit health-related behavior, attitudes, and feelings and indicates degrees to which students adhere to a healthy lifestyle. Publisher: Student Development Associates, Inc. and is available from Appalachian State University. For more information: http://sdtla.appstate.edu/

## F. Related Websites

| | |
|---|---|
| Harvard School of Public health, College Alcohol Study | http://www.hsph.harvard.edu/cas/ |
| National Center Education Statistics | http://www.nces.ep.gov/ |
| ACPA: College Educators International | http://www.nche.acpa.org/ |
| American College Health Association | http://www.acha.org/ |
| Chronicle of Higher Education. | http://www.chronicle.com/ |
| Association of Student Personnel Administrators | http://www.naspa.org/. National/ |
| Higher Education Center | http://www.edc.org/hec/ |
| National Center for Education Statistics. | http://www.nces.ed.gov/ |

## G. References

Bandura, A. (1977) *Social learning theory.* Englewood Cliffs, NJ: Prentice Hall.

Chickering, A. W. (1969). *Education and identity.* San Francisco: Jossey-Bass.

Fetro, J. V. & Drolet, J. C. (2000). *Personal and social competence: Strategies for communication, decision-making, goal setting, stress management.* Santa Cruz, CA: ETR Associates.

Kohlberg, L. (1971). Stages of moral development as a basis for moral education. In C. Beck, B. S., Crittenden, & E. V., Sullivan (Eds.). *Moral education: Interdisciplinary approaches* (pp. 23-92). Toronto: University of Toronto Press.

McLeroy, K. R., Bibeau, D. Steckler, A., Glanz, K. (1988). An ecological perspective on health promotion programs. *Health Education Quarterly* 15:351-377.

Underhile, R. (2000). *Examining capacity and readiness for establishing and sustaining a coordinated school health program at the college level: A case study.* Unpublished doctoral dissertation, Southern Illinois University, Carbondale.

## H. Recommended reading

Advisory Committee on Immunization Practices. (2000). Meningococcal disease and college students: Recommendations of the Advisory Committee on Immunization Practices (ACIP). *MMWR Morbidity and Morality Weekly Report*, 49, 11-20.

American College Health Association. (2005). *Standards of practice for health promotion in higher education.* Retrieved May 30, 2006, from http://www.acha.org

American College Health Association. (2005). *Vision into action: Tools for professional and program development based on the standards of practice for health promotion in higher education.* Baltimore: Author.

American College Health Association. (2004). *National College Health Assessment Report*. Retrieved May 30, 2006, from http://www.acha.org/projects_programs/assessment.cfm

American College Health Association. (2002). *Healthy campus 2010 making it happen*. Baltimore: Author.

American College Health Association. (1999). *Guidelines for a college health program*. Baltimore: Author.

Bartholomew, L. K., Parcel, G. S., Kok, G., & Gottlieb, N. H. (2001). *Intervention mapping: Designing theory and evidence-based health promotion programs*. Mountain View, CA: Mayfield Publishing Company.

Bransford, J., Brown, A., & Cocking, R. (Eds). (2000). *How people learn: Brain, mind experience and school: Expanded edition*. Washington, DC: National Academy Press.

Centers for Disease Control and Prevention. (1997). Youth risk behavior surveillance: National College Health Risk Behavior Survey-United States, *Morbidity & Mortality Weekly Report CDC Surveillance Summary*, 46(6), 1-56.

Chronicle of Higher Education. Almanac issue (2005–2006), http://chronicle.com/free/almanac/2005/notes/notes.htm

Caufield, S. (Ed). (2005). Health education and health promotion: Primary prevention and student health. *Student Health Spectrum*. Retrieved May 30, 2006 from http://www.chickering.com

Chickering, A. W., Dalton J. C., & Stamm, L. (2005). *Encouraging authenticity and spirituality in higher education*. San Fransisco: Jossey-Bass.

Christmas, W. A. & Dorman, J. M. (1996). The story of college health and hygiene: Thomas A. Storey, MD (1875-1943). *Journal of American College Health*, 45 (1), 27-34.

Christmas, W. A., & Berkowitz, S. D. (1989). Sexual behavior and the structure of STDs on a college campus. *Journal of American College Health*, 38, 40.

Crihfield, C. (1995). College health: A nursing perspective. *Journal of American College Health*, 43(6), 253-257.

Elster, A.B. & Kuznets, N. J. (Eds.). (1994). *AMA guidelines for adolescent preventive services (GAPS): Recommendations and rationale*. Baltimore: Williams & Wilkins.

Fabiano, P. & Swinford, P. (2004). Serving higher education communities with health promotion. *American Journal of Health Promotion*, 18(5), 6-7.

Goldstein, M. A. (2002). Preparing adolescent patients for college. *Current Opinion in Pediatrics*, 14, 384.

Hussar, W. J. (2005) *Projections of Education Statistics to 2014* (NCES 2005-074). U.S. Washington, DC: U.S. Government Printing Office.

Jackson, M., & Weinstein, H. (1997). The importance of healthy communities of higher education. *Journal of American College Health*, 45, 237.

Kadison, R. D., & DiGeronimo, T. F. (2004). *College of the overwhelmed: The campus mental health crisis and what to do about it*. San Francisco: Jossey-Bass.

Keeling, R.P. (Ed). (2006). *Learning reconsidered 2: Implementing a campus-wide focus on the student experience*. Washington, DC: American College Personnel Association and National Association of Student Personnel Administrators.

Keeling, R. P. (2004). Population level prevention in practice. *Leadership Exchange* 2(1),14-17.

Keeling, R. P. (Ed). (2004). *Learning reconsidered: A campus-wide focus on the student experience.* Washington, DC: American College Personnel Association and National Association of Student Personnel Administrators.

Keeling, R. P. (2002). Why college health matters. [Editorial] *Journal of American College Health*, 50, 261.

Keeling, R. P. (2000). Beyond the campus clinic: A holistic approach to student health. *AAC&U Peer Review*, 2(3), 13-18.

Minkler, M. (1999). Personal responsibility for health? A review of the arguments and evidence at century's end. *Health Education & Behavior*, 26, 121-140.

Modeste, N. (1996). *Dictionary of public health promotion and education: Terms and concepts.* Thousand Oaks, CA: Sage.

National Association of Student Personnel Administrators and American College Health Association. (2004). *Leadership for a healthy campus: an ecological approach to student success.* Washington, CD: Author.

National Association of Student Personnel Administrators and American College Health Association. (1998). *Principles of good practice for student affairs: statement and inventories.* Washington, DC: Author.

Patrick, K. (Ed.). (1992). *Principles and practices of student health: Volume three: College health.* Oakland, CA: Third Party Publishing Company

Patrick, K. (1988). Student health: Medical care within institutions of higher education. *Journal of the American Medical Association*, 260, 3301-3305.

Rimsza, E. M., Kirk, G. M. (2005). Common medical problems of the college student. *Pediatric Clinics of North America.* 52, 9.

Swinford, P. L. (2002). Advancing the health of students: A rationale for college health programs. *Journal of American College Health*, 50, 309.

Task Force of the National Advisory Council on Alcohol Abuse and Alcoholism. (2002). *A call to action: Changing the culture of drinking at U.S. colleges.* National Institutes of Health, U.S. Department of Health and Human Services. Retrieved May 30, 2006 from http://www.collegedrinkingprevention.gov.

U.S. Department of Human Services. (2000). *Healthy People 2010.* Retrieved May 30, 2006, from http://www.healthypeople.gov/Publications/2nd ed

Wechsler, H., Seibring, M., Liu, I. C., & Ahl, M. (2004). Colleges respond to student binge drinking: Reducing student demand or limiting access. *Journal of American College Health.* 2004; 52(4), 159-168.

# Independence

"[Independence] has to do with a sense of one's own identity. It involves an ability to act independently and to exert some control over one's environment, and includes a sense of task mastery, internal locus of control, self-agency, and self-efficacy." (Benard, 1995, p. 67)

## A. Introduction

Educational philosophers like Whitehead (1929), Dewey (1916), and Cardinal Newman (1907) asserted that education should produce more independent persons. Such educated persons should demonstrate increasing levels of independence from the influence of others including parents, peers, and institutions.

Studies concerning independence focus on the "extent to which college students' susceptibility to external influences changes over time" (Pascarella & Terenzini, 2005, p. 222). Though various theoretical considerations and conceptual frameworks exist, the underlying constructs share an emphasis on the degree to which students feel in control of their own lives. In this way, independence is closely related to, if not synonymous with, other affective outcomes such as locus of control and self-efficacy.

As Dewey and others suggested, developing students' independence is an important outcome of college. Most studies provide clear evidence of the significantly positive effect of college on one's independence from others and locus of control. For example, college students who indicate higher levels of self-efficacy tend to exhibit stronger academic achievement than do their less effective peers (Multon, Brown, & Lent, 1991). Also students who are internally directed are more likely to have higher academic achievements than those who believe their success is a function of chance or luck (Perry, 1991). Studies often depend on theoretical assumptions that tend to reflect dominant cultures and values versus understanding the distinctive nature of other cultural perspectives. Sebsequent literature on independence recognizes the importance of balancing responsibility to others and community with mastery of one's life (Belenky, Clichy, Goldberger, & Tarule, 1986; Chickering & Reisser, 1993; Gilligan, 1982; Noddings, 1984).

Independence is one of the 16 learning domains identified by the CAS for the Advancement of Standards in Higher Education (CAS). Examples of achievement indicators are exhibiting self-reliant behaviors and functioning autonomously. Given that independence is an important outcome of formal education, particularly at the postsecondary level, all educators should be sure that their work promotes students' independence.

## B. Theoretical Contexts for Learning and Development

The opening quote by Benard (1995) sheds light on the theoretical underpinnings of learning and development in this domain. Independence is, at least in part, about identity as well as a balanced interpersonal foundation. "Moving through autonomy toward interdependence" is one of the seven vectors proposed by Chickering (Chickering, 1969; Chickering & Reisser, 1993). This phase of development is characterized by increased emotional and instrumental independence, which includes self-directedness and freedom from the need for validation of others. A clear sense of identity leads toward self-acceptance, self-reliance, and ultimately an understanding of one's connectedness with others.

In addition, to the extent that independence is related to identity development, it may refer to elements of life span theory as well. Erikson (1959/1980, 1963, 1968) was the first to suggest a lifespan framework for identity development. He described eight stages associated with the establishment of identity that are characterized by a central developmental crisis. Each crisis must be resolved successfully by balancing internal self with one's environment. Stage 2 is particularly relevant to development in this domain as it focuses on the conflict between autonomy versus shame and doubt. Successful resolution of this stage results in increasing levels of independence.

Developing independence is an important aspect of psychosocial development for all persons. Josselson (1987) referred to this process in women as identity achievement. Women exhibiting identity achievement have more mature and equitable relationships with parents and others to form their own image of self. This may also be related to the later stages of racial identity development as proposed by Cross (1995) and Helms (1995). Baxter Magolda's (2001, 2003) recent work on self- authorship is informative here as well.

## C. Relevant Variables

- exhibits self-reliant behaviors
- exhibits ability to function interdependently
- manages time effectively
- makes decisions and acts in congruence with personal values
- identifies personal, work, and lifestyle values
- manages personal finances well
- accepts supervision as needed
- functions without need for constant reassurance from others
- acknowledges personal strengths and weaknesses
- sets and pursues individual goals

This list of variables is by no means an exhaustive list of all of the relevant variables associated with independence. Rather, it is intended to provide a point of departure for thinking about assessing the dimensions of learning related to independence.

Because it is imperative to identify variables early in the assessment process, this list provides the reader with several variables that might be used. As a general rule, the criterion (or dependent) variable essentially answers the question: What am I measuring? The predictor (or independent) variables, on the other hand, are those factors that are controlled or manipulated rather than observed. The predictor variable is often a grouping variable (for example, gender or year in college) and is the factor that is thought to be causal. For example, in most cases the dependent variable is the learning outcome while "manages time effectively" may be one of the independent variables.

## D. Assessment Examples

Dr. Beema Self was recently appointed as the Associate Dean of Multicultural Affairs at Arizona City University (ACU). ACU is a large, public institution that serves a large number of American Indian students. In her position, Dr. Self is responsible for promoting the academic success of African American, Hispanic, and American Indian students.

At a recent meeting, an academic dean stressed his frustration with the low number of American Indian students who persisted to receive their undergraduate degree from ACU within five years. The provost acknowledged the dean's concern and moved to form a committee that would investigate the factors that influence academic persistence of Native American students at ACU. Dr. Self was appointed chair of the committee.

At her first committee meeting, Dr. Self led a discussion to establish the central research question. Per the provost's suggestion, the guiding question was: What factors influence academic persistence of American Indian college students in general? And, to what extent do these factors influence the academic persistence of Native American undergraduates at ACU?

To answer the first question, the assessment team conducted an extensive literature review and found that family encouragement, academic preparation and aspirations, perceived discrimination, social integration, interaction with faculty and staff, valuing of education, academic performance, and independence influence academic success of American Indian students. To investigate the second question, they considered the following approaches:

1. Quantitative: After looking through the files that she inherited from the former dean, Dr. Self realized that the problem of academic persistence of American Indian students had been investigated five years prior. In the earlier study, data were collected on the academic behaviors and attitudes of comparable undergraduates at the University. The team decided to use the existing data as a starting place for the assessment project.

   At the next committee meeting, the team brainstormed how they might design the study to examine the effect of behaviors and attitudes on academic persistence. To do this, they needed to gather information on the current academic status of those who were surveyed five years ago. Using student ID numbers and with permission from the institution's Human Subjects Committee, the researchers contacted the registrar's office for information on degrees earned and current educational status.

   Of the original 292 participants, only two were eliminated because their enrollment data were not accessible. Those who had obtained a bachelor's degree or were currently enrolled were designated as "persisters" while those who were no longer enrolled and had not obtained a degree were categorized as "non-persisters." Of the 290 Native American students in the resulting sample, 52% were persisters and 48% were non-persisters.

   The researchers used a theoretical framework to select items from the original survey to include in the current study. Using Tinto's (1975) model of attrition, the researchers selected items that seemed to reflect elements of Tinto's theory and those items that pertain to issues faced by students of color. In the end, 40 items were selected and subjected to confirmatory factor analysis. Six factors were extracted and given names similar to the constructs of Tinto's theory: social integration, valuing education, family encouragement, and independence to name a few. They also added each student's GPA as a measure of academic performance.

   The main research question was tested by discriminant analysis and multivariate analysis of variance (MANOVA). Discriminant analysis was used to test whether group membership (persister or non-persister) could be determined by the seven factors. In particular, the researchers were interested in the ability of "independence" to predict group membership. Multiple analyses of variance tests were used to assess differences between the groups across all seven factors.

2. Qualitative: To prepare for a study of student persistence of American Indians, Dr. Self began reading reports on the status of American Indian students in education. A recent report by the Department of Education noted that quantitative studies often depend on theoretical assumptions that tend to reflect dominant cultures and values versus understanding the distinctive nature of other cultural perspectives. The report recommended the use of qualitative methods to complement quantitative data.

With this in mind, Dr. Self encouraged the committee to consider a mixed methods approach to the study at the next meeting and asked Dr. Questa Nair, professor of educational research, for her insights on an appropriate technique. Dr. Nair recommended that the team use *mixed methods*, a study that uses both qualitative and quantitative data collection and analysis in either a parallel or sequential manner (Jones, Torres, & Arminio, 2006) where "The mixing occurs in the methods section of the study" (Tashakkori & Teddlie, 2003, p. 11). Because the analysis of the methods are usually done separately, this type of study does not always require the consideration of distinctions between the constructivist or positivist paradigms associated with qualitative and quantitative research (Tashakkori & Teddlie).

For the qualitative portion, a grounded theory methodology was selected in order to offer a theoretical model of how the notion of independence influences American Indian persistence. One-on-one interviews were used to gather rich, thick data from American Indian students at ACU. With Dr. Nair's help, the researchers adopted the following criteria for sample selection: (a) students had lived on a reservation for the majority of their school years prior to beginning college, (b) had parents who both identified as Native Americans, (c) were college seniors in good academic standing, and (d) had been enrolled in college for no more than five years.

Researchers conducted several one-on-one interviews with 15 American Indian students over the fall and spring semesters. A list of interview questions was used to help interviewers guide the discussion and avoid leading questions. Specifically, two questions asked students to consider the ways in which collectivism and independence affects their lives. During the interview, participants were asked to complete an informed consent form. Each interview was recorded, transcribed, and then interpreted by the researchers using interpretive qualitative methods under the advice of Dr. Nair. First, researchers read through all transcripts to approximate the meanings of events. The team continued to read transcripts with a goal of uncovering progressively deeper understandings of the text using a structured sequence of codes and categories as described by Glasser and Strauss (1967, 1999). From this structure, a theoretical model was created that informed the committee about how independence influences these students and their experiences at college.

## E. Available Instruments

A word of caution—be certain that these instruments yield the type of data that you need to assess your program's effectiveness. To do this, first determine what you want to know and then search for the instrument that will provide you with such information. Do not do the reverse. If none of these instruments yield the kind of data that you are interested in, you are advised to develop your own instrument to meet your specific needs.

*Pathways to Independence* by Dorothy M. Jeffree and Sally Cheseldine, n.d.
- Measures skills that influence personal and social independence.
- Publisher: Hodder & Stoughton Educational, 338 Euston Road, London NW1 3BH, England
- For more information: www.hoddertests.co.uk

*Career Maturity Inventory (CMI)* by John O. Crites, n.d.
- Measures the degree of maturity of attitudes and abilities that are necessary for career decision making.
- Publisher: Chronicle Guidance Publications, Inc., 66 Aurora Street, Moravia, NY 13118-1190.
- For more information: www.unl.edu/buros

*Family Environment Scale (FES)* by Rudolf M. Moos and Bernice S. Moos, n.d.
- Measures family members' perceptions of the social environment.
- Publisher: CPP, Inc., 3803 East Bayshore Road, Palo Alto, CA 94303.
- For more information: www.cpp-db.com

*Miller Psychological Independence Scale* by Harold J. Miller, n.d.
- Measures an individual's psychological independence along a dependent-independent continuum.
- Publisher: Meta Development LLC, 4313 Garnet Street, Regina, Saskatchewan S4S 6J8, Canada.
- For more information: www.unl.edu/buros

*Developing Autonomy Task of the Student Developmental Task and Lifestyle Assessment (SDTLA)* by R. B. Winston, T. K. Miller, and D. L. Cooper, 1997.
- Autonomy is defined by four subtasks: Emotional Autonomy, Interdependence, Academic Autonomy, and Instrumental Autonomy.
- Publisher: Appalachian State University, Boone, NC 28608.
- For more information: http://www.sdtla.appstate.edu

Several purpose statements were adapted from those produced by the Buros Institute of Mental Measurements Test Reviews Online: www.unl.edu/buros

## F. Related Websites

| | |
|---|---|
| Personal autonomy | http://plato.stanford.edu/entries/personal-autonomy/ |
| Theory of Autonomy | http://www.theihs.org/libertyguide/hsr/hsr.php/33.html |
| Functional Independence Handbook | http://webpages.charter.net/fishscales/index.html |
| Autonomy | http://www-personal.umich.edu/~velleman/Practical_Reflection/chapter6.html |
| Autonomy in Moral Philosophy | http://plato.stanford.edu/entries/autonomy-moral/ |

It should be noted that the list consists of "autonomy-focused" websites largely. However, independence is much more than mere autonomy and the author encourages readers to recognize the fact that independence is more closely related to interdependence in their assessment work.

## G. References

Benard, B. (1995). Fostering resiliency in urban schools. In B. Williams (Ed.), *Closing the achievement gap: A vision to guide change in beliefs and practice*. Oak Brook, IL: Research for Better Schools and North Central Regional Educational Laboratory.

Baxter Magolda, M. B. (2001). *Making their own way*. Sterling, VA: Stylus.

Baxter Magolda, M. B. (2003). Identity and learning: Student affairs' role in transforming higher education. *Journal of College Student Development*, 44(2,) 231-246.

Belenky, M. F., Clinchy, B. M., Goldberger, N. R., & Tarule, J. M. (1986). *Women's way of knowing: The development of self, voice, and mind*. New York: Basic Books.

Cardinal Newman, J. H. (1907). *The idea of a university: Defined and illustrated*. New York: Longmans, Green, and Company.

Chickering, A. W. (1969). *Education and identity*. San Francisco: Jossey-Bass.

Chickering, A. W., & Reisser, L. (1993). *Education and identity* (2nd ed.). San Francisco: Jossey-Bass.

Cross, W. E. (1995). The psychology of Nigrescence: Revising the Cross model. In J. G. Ponterotto, J. M. Casas, L. A. Suzuki, & C. M. Alexander (Eds.), *Handbook of multicultural counseling* (pp. 93-122). Thousand Oaks, CA: Sage.

Dewey, J. (1916). *Education and democracy*. New York: MacMillan Company.

Erikson, E. H. (1963). *Childhood and society* (2nd ed.). New York: Norton.

Erikson, E. H. (1968). *Identity: Youth and crisis*. New York: Norton.

Erikson, E. H. (1980). *Identity and the life cycle*. New York: Norton. (Original work published 1959)

Gilligan, C. (1982). *In a different voice*. Cambridge, MA: Harvard University Press.

Glaser, B. G. & Strauss, A.L. (1967/1999). *Discovery of grounded theory: Strategies for qualitative research*. Chicago: Aldine.

Helms, J. E. (1995). An update of Helms's White and People of Color racial idenity models. In J. G. Ponterotto, J. M. Casias, L. A. Suzuki, & C. M. Alexander (Eds.), *Handbook of multicultural counseling* (pp. 181-198). Thousand Oaks, CA: Sage.

Jones, S. R., Torres, V. & Arminio, J. (2006). *Negotiating the complexities of qualitative research in higher education*. New York: Routledge.

Josselson, R. (1987). *Finding herself: Pathways to identity development in women*. San Francisco: Jossey-Bass.

Multon, K., Brown, S., & Lent, R. (1991). Relation of self-efficacy beliefs to academic outcomes: A meta-analytic investigation. *Journal of Counseling Psychology*, 38, 30-38.

Noddings, N. (1984). *Caring: A feminine approach to ethics and moral education*. Berekley, CA: University of California Press.

Pascarella, E. T., & Terenzini, P. T. (2005). *How college affects students: A third decade of research*. San Francisco: Jossey-Bass.

Perry, R. (1991). Perceived control in college students: Implications for instruction in higher education. In J. Smart (Ed.), *Higher education: Handbook of theory and research* (Vol. 7, pp. 1-56). New York: Agathon.

Tashakkori, A. and Teddlie, C. (2003). *Handbook of mixed methods in social & behavioral research*. Thousand Oaks, CA: Sage.

Tinto, V. (1975). Dropout from higher education: A theoretical synthesis of recent research. *Review of Educational Research*, 45(1), 89-125.

Whitehead, A. N. (1929). *The aims of education and other essays*. New York: MacMillan Company.

## H. Recommended Reading

Heath, D. H. (1991). *Fulfilling lives: Paths to maturity and success*. San Francisco: Jossey-Bass.

# Intellectual Growth

## A. Introduction

Intellectual growth is one of the learning and development domains identified by the Council for the Advancement of Standards in Higher Education (CAS). Intellectual development refers to increasing complexity of thought and ideas. It is often confused with cognitive development. But, the two are not entirely synonymous as intellectual development is often related to knowledge acquisition while cognitive development refers to changes in the *way* a person thinks. Relevant student learning and development outcomes of intellectual development range from expressed appreciation for fine arts to obtaining a college degree.

Intellectual development is primarily and fundamentally what college is all about. The historic purpose of college is to develop the mind and being of learners (Perry, 1981). CAS advises that all functional areas must be: (a) responsive to the needs of individuals, special populations, and communities, (b) reflective of developmental and demographic profiles of the student population, and (c) based on theories and knowledge of learning and human development. It is expected that all functional area programs will emphasize learning and work to identify relevant learning outcomes. By using CAS functional area standards and guidelines, program leaders can assess student learning and development relative to intellectual development.

## B. Theoretical Contexts for Learning and Development

Several theories have been posited to explain intellectual growth and development. The works of Piaget (1952), Perry (1968, 1978, 1981), and Kohlberg (1969; 1971) are important and relevant to this domain. Collectively, these theories are referred to as cognitive-structural theories. Cognitive structural theories focus on changes in the *way* people think rather than the *content* of their thinking.

Cognitive structural theories are influenced largely by the early work of Jean Piaget (1950; 1952) often referred to as the father of cognitive-structural developmental theories. Piaget studied young children—including his own—to understand how meaning is made and how reasoning occurs. His theory consisted of four basic stages: sensory motor stage, pre-operations stage, operations, and formal operations. He determined that development continues after childhood.

Based on Piaget's work, intellectual development is concerned with knowledge acquisition and meaning making. Development, from this perspective, is marked by moving from simple meanings and understandings toward increasingly complex integration and differentiation.

Perry's (1968; 1978; 1981) theory relates to meaning making processes. It consists of nine positions that can be grouped into four categories: dualism, multiplicity, relativism, and commitment to relativism. Like most cognitive-structural theories, his work is characterized by a logical progression from simple meanings to more complex modes of reasoning. For example, duality suggests that one right answer exists while multiplicity acknowledges diverse views. Relativism highlights the fact that knowledge is much more qualitative than dualistic and that all knowledge is contextually defined (Perry, 1968). Because these early theories emphasized the intellectual development of men, Belenky, Clinchy, Goldberger, and Tarule (1986) utilized Perry's methodology to study a sample of women. They noted differences in the ways women come to know. In particular, they noted silence and connected knowing as experiences particular to women. Baxter Magolda (1992) also used Perry's methodology except in a longitudinal study. She noted four approaches to learning: absolute, transitional, independent, and contextual that related to learner and teacher expectations and means of evaluation. Baxter Magolda noted gender-related patterns in the first three of these approaches.

Another unique feature of cognitive-structural theories is that they consist of invariant sequential stages through which all persons must progress if normal development is to occur. Developmental stages are organized hierarchically. That is, the cognitive structure associated with each successive stage is more integrated and complex than the stage before. Latter stages incorporate higher forms of thinking and more complex modes of reasoning.

The Reflective Judgment Model (RJM) proposed by King and Kitchener (1994) is used to understand the process of and rationale for development of different forms of reasoning. The main tenet of their model holds that a person's assumptions about what and how something can be known provide a lens for framing problems and responding to them. The model is applicable to all persons in late childhood through adulthood. It consists of seven stages that are described as a movement from "knowledge as absolute" to "knowledge resulting from a process of reasonable inquiry." Generally, stages 1-3 are collectively pre-reflective thinking stages, stages 4-5 are quasi-reflective thinking stages, and 6-7 are reflective thinking stages. Fundamentally, their work focuses on how people decide what to believe about "ill-structured problems," a term coined by the authors.

Finally, there is additional current theoretical work in this area. Baxter Magolda continues her research using the same sample from her dissertation study and has promoted the importance of self-authorship (2001, 2003).

By understanding cognitive-structural theories, educators can better understand how students think and learn. With such knowledge, educators and student affairs professionals can be more intentional in providing instruction and services that influence students' intellect and knowledge acquisition. In addition, by understanding the theoretical context of intellectual development, one can more easily and effectively assess the effect of a program on learning and development in this domain.

## C. Relevant Variables

- thinks critically
- uses complex information to make decisions
- obtains a degree
- applies prior information to a new situation or setting
- writes coherently
- produces personal and educational goal statements
- solves problems
- uses information from a variety of sources to make decisions/opinion
- completes a course
- expresses appreciation for literature, fine arts, math, or science, etc.
- speaks fluently and effectively
- utilizes one's own informed views in writing essays, poems, speeches, etc.
- gains knowledge

This list of variables is by no means an all-inclusive list of the relevant variables associated with intellectual development. It is intended to provide a general starting point for thinking about assessing the effectiveness of a program relative to intellectual development. It is important to identify the dependent and independent variables early in the assessment process. The dependent variable essentially answers the question: What am I measuring? The independent variables are the factors that are controlled or vary, often referred to as a "treatment." For example, in most cases, the dependent variable might be "intellectual development" or some form of ability or skill. In other cases, intellectual ability or growth may serve as an independent variable that is related to the dependent variable.

## D. Assessment Examples

After hearing students debate current issues in the lounge of the multicultural center, Dr. Juan B. Smart decided to create a program that would increase students' knowledge of current events. His concern is that much of what he overhears is students' repeating rumors and students' not listening to each other's views. The participants ranged from second- to senior-year college students and represented a variety of academic majors. Dr. Smart hosted bi-weekly discussions on current events. He also invited students on the institution's debate team to assist him in mentoring and instructing students on how to argue an informed point of view to a multicultural audience. They also discussed with members of the debate team cultural influences on debate and discourse. Next, Dr. Smart decided to assess the effectiveness of his program to determine whether students were growing intellectually. To do this, he did the following:

1. Quantitative: Dr. Smith organized a public debate inviting students from outside his group to also participate. He invited several faculty and student affairs professionals to serve as responders of the debate. The topic of the debate was "The question of the influence of race in the response to hurricane Katrina." Also, students were to offer creative solutions of how college students could assist in the elimination of poverty in the U.S. He created an instrument to evaluate the effectiveness of students' arguments and their knowledge on the topic. The assessment consisted of three sections: knowledge of the topic, oral debate, and problem solving. Each section consisted of five questions. Items in the sections were designed to measure the ability of students to use knowledge creation and critical thought to solve complex problems and on how and whether their point of view was grounded in evidence such as facts, feelings, experiences, and values in an organized and thoughtful fashion. Scores were compared between students in his bi-weekly meetings and other students.

2. Qualitative: Dr. Smart decided to conduct a phenomenological assessment studying students' lived experience of being involved in the program. He specifically asked students to write about how they experienced the program. What do they know now that they didn't know before? How did they experience this new knowing? How did they formulate an argument before the program, after? How did they organize their reasoning for their point of view before, during, and after the program? How did they experience their meetings, the public debate? How did they experience entering a discussion or debate with people of varying views before, during, and after the program? How did they experience changing their points of view? Dr. Smart looked for and then analyzed common themes exposing hidden meaning in students' lived experiences.

## E. Available Instruments

A word of caution—be certain that these instruments yield the type of data that you need to assess your program's effectiveness. To do this, first determine what you want to know and then search for the measurement tool that will provide such information. Do not do the reverse. If none of the available instruments will yield the kind of data in which you are interested, you are advised to create your own instrument to meet your needs.

*Watson-Glaser Critical Thinking Appraisal (WGCTA)* by Berger, 1985.
- Designed to measure numerical and thinking skills. Critical thinking measures include drawing inferences, recognizing assumptions, argument evaluation, deductive reasoning, and logical interpretation.
- Publisher: Get Feedback, Inc.
- For more information: www.getfeedback.net

*Cornell Critical Thinking Test (CCTT)* by Malcolm, 1992.
- Measures students' critical thinking abilities. The test can be used to teach critical thinking skills.
- Publisher: The Critical Thinking Co.
- For more information: www.criticalthinking.com

*California Critical Thinking Skills Test* by Michael, 1995.
- Critical thinking test designed to assess an individual's or group's critical thinking and reasoning skills. Also used to gather information for program evaluation and research on critical thinking skills development. For use with adults in college and professional schools.
- Publisher: Insight Assessment, Inc.
- For more information: www.insightassessment.com/test-cctst.html

*Collegiate Assessment of Academic Proficiency (CAAP)* by Own, 1998.
- Measures students' achievement levels on a group and individual basis. Designed to enable institutions to measure, evaluate, and optimize the outcomes of their educational program.
- Publisher: ACT, Inc.
- For more information: www.act.org/caap

Several purpose statements were adapted from those produced by the Buros Institute of Mental Measurements Test Reviews Online: www.unl.edu/buros

## F. Related Websites

| | |
|---|---|
| The Perry Network | www.perrynetwork.org |
| Perry's Nine Positions | http://www.cs.buffalo.edu/~rapaport/perry.positions.html |
| Cognitive Structural Theories/Piaget | http://tip.psychology.org/piaget.html |
| Epistemology | http://www.educationau.edu.au/archives/cp/04g.htm |

## G. References

Baxter Magolda, M. B. (1992). *Knowing and reasoning in college: Gender–related patterns in students' intellectual development.* San Francisco: Jossey-Bass.

Baxter Magolda, M. B. (2001). *Making their own way.* Sterling, VA: Stylus.

Baxter Magolda, M. B. (2003). Identity and learning: Student affairs' role in transforming higher education. *Journal of College Student Development*, 44(2), 231-246.

Belenky, M. F., Clinchy, B. M., Goldberger, N. R., & Tarule, J. M. (1986). *Women's ways of knowing: The development of self, voice, and mind.* New York: Basic Books.

King, P. M. & Kitchener, K. S. (1994). *Developing reflective judgment: Understanding and promoting intellectual growth and critical thinking in adolescents.* San Francisco; Jossey-Bass.

Kohlberg, L. (1969). Stage and sequence: The cognitive developmental approach to socialization. In D. A. Goslin (Ed.), *Handbook of socialization theory and research* (pp. 347-480). Chicago: Rand McNally.

Kohlberg, L. (1971). Stages of moral development as a basis for moral education. In C. Beck, B. S. Crittenden, & E. V. Sullivan (Eds.), *Moral education: Interdisciplinary approaches* (pp. 23-92). Toronto, Canada: University of Toronto Press.

Perry, W. G., Jr. (1968). *Forms of intellectual and ethical development in the college years: A scheme.* New York: Holt, Rinehart & Winston.

Perry, W. G., Jr. (1978). Sharing in the costs of growth. In C. A. Parker (Ed.), *Encouraging development in college students* (pp. 267-273). Minneapolis: University of Minnesota Press.

Perry, W. G., Jr. (1981). Cognitive and ethical growth: The making of meaning. In A. W. Chickering & Associates (Eds.), *The modern American college: Responding to the new realities of diverse students and a changing society* (pp. 76-116). San Francisco: Jossey-Bass.

Piaget, J. (1950). *The psychology of intelligence* (M. Piercy & D. E. Berlyne, Trans.). London: Routledge & Kegan Paul.

Piaget, J. (1952). *The origins of intelligence in children.* New York: International Universities Press.

## H. Recommended Reading

Baxter Magolda, M. B. (1987). Comparing open-ended interviews and standardized measures of intellectual development. *Journal of College Student Personnel, 28,* 443-448.

Baxter Magolda, M. B. (1992). *Knowing and reasoning in college: Gender-related patterns in students' intellectual development.* San Francisco: Jossey-Bass.

Baxter Magolda, M. B. (1995). The integration of relational and impersonal knowing in young adults' epistemological development. *Journal of College Student Development, 36,* 205-216.

Guba, E. G., & Lincoln, Y. S. (1994). Competing paradigms in qualitative research. In N. K. Denzin & Y. S. Lincoln (Eds.), *Handbook of qualitative research* (pp. 105-117). Thousand Oaks, CA: Sage.

King, P. M. (1990). Assessing development from a cognitive developmental perspective. In D. G. Creamer (Ed.), *College student development: Theory and practice for the 1990s* (pp. 81-98). Alexandria, VA: American College Personnel Association.

Perry, W. G., Jr. (1977). Intellectual and ethical forms of development. *Pupil Personnel Services Journal, 6* (1), 61-68.

# Leadership Development

## A. Introduction

The Council for the Advancement of Standards in Higher Education (CAS) published *The Book of Professional Standards for Higher Education* that offers standards for over 30 functional areas in higher education. The CAS functional area standards and guidelines serve as a reference for program leaders who are interested in outcomes assessment. Outcomes assessment primarily focuses on student learning and development. In that way, the CAS standards provide educators with a set of relevant and desirable learning objectives related to a specific learning domain.

Educators and program leaders are encouraged to: (1) set clear objectives for all programs and services and (2) to provide evidence of achievement of student learning and development outcomes. Each framework is designed to be an aide to educators who are interested in learning and development outcomes assessment and to professionals charged with of assessing student learning.

Leadership development is one of the 16 student learning and development outcome domains identified by CAS. Indicators of leadership development include the ability to articulate a leadership philosophy or style, serve in a leadership position in a student organization, comprehend the dynamics of a group, exhibit democratic principles as a leader, and exhibit the ability to visualize a group purpose and desired outcomes.

Leadership abilities can be intentionally learned. In fact, leadership development may well be one of the most fundamental and historic outcomes of college, as most colonial institutions were established to provide formal education to wealthy men who became state and religious leaders (Lucas, 1994). Leadership development remains today as a relevant and desirable learning outcome that is often nourished through co-curricular involvement (Astin & Astin, 2000; Pascarella & Terenzini, 2005).

Like any other skill, leadership has to be learned and practiced (Komives, Lucas, & McMahon, 1998). By identifying specific learning tasks and goals associated with leadership development, one can intentionally create opportunities which foster such development in college. Astin (1993) stressed the importance of involvement and leadership as it increases students' ability to make a difference in society both locally and globally. His thoughts echo the comments of Morgan, "the degree of democracy existing in college will largely influence the amount exercised by the graduate later in his community and if anything like democracy is to survive in America it must have a school for training" (1960, pp. 116-117)

In the 1980s, colleges and universities established specific leadership development programs and curricula for students. A belief that leadership was taught through theories, experiences, and interactions replaced an earlier view that merely attending college created a leader (Boccia, 1997). This paradigm shift made student leadership development a priority and gave it a place within the curriculum (Bennett & Shayner, 1988).

With the move of leadership development from the periphery occupied largely by the extracurricular to the center of education, several other changes were prompted. First, leadership development became an appropriate learning objective and outcome of educational experiences. Second, theorists began to posit explanations relative to leadership development as a learning process. Third, educators became interested in assessing leadership development as a viable learning outcome.

The sections that follow provide useful information to educators about the theoretical underpinnings of leadership development, a list of relevant variables or indicators that relate to leadership development, and examples of how to measure such development using multiple methods of assessment.

## B. Theoretical Contexts for Learning and Development

Leadership is regarded as one of the most widely studied but least understood phenomena (Burns, 1978). Rogers (2003) offered a description differentiating "conventional views of leadership" (emphasizing influencing others) from "alternative views of leadership" (servant, transforming, and critical) (pp. 450-453). The post-industrial leadership scholarship includes the relational, character-focused social constructions of leadership embracing values, ethical practices, inclusion, and collaborative practices that lead to shared vision.

One way to broaden the notion of leadership is to use theoretical leadership development models. One such model examines how leadership can be enhanced in college students is the Social Change Model of Leadership Development. This model was created in 1996 by an ensemble of leadership educators with principle investigators Alexander and Helen Astin at the University of California, Los Angeles Higher Education Research Institute (HERI), and funded by the Eisenhower Leadership Program (Astin, 1996). This model suggested that leadership is a values-based process of identifying a need and working collaboratively with others to meet that need and accomplish other goals. The Social Change Model addresses seven values of development that ultimately result in change. These are: consciousness of self, congruence, commitment, collaboration, common purpose, controversy with civility, and citizenship (Higher Education Research Institute, 1996)

The Social Change Model, also known as the Seven Cs, is considered to be an inclusive model that views leadership as a process rather than a position. The Social Change Model views leadership development from three perspectives: the individual, the group, and the community/society. Each perspective relates to several key values.

Within the individual perspective lie the *conscious of self, congruence, and commitment* principles. The conscious of self principle refers to being aware of the values, emotions, attitudes, and beliefs that motivate a person to take action, including how one understands others.

The congruence principle means thinking, feeling, and behaving with consistency, genuineness, authenticity, and honesty toward others. The commitment principle suggests intensity and duration. It requires significant involvement and investment of one's self in the activity and its intended outcomes (Allen & Cherry, 2000; Astin, 1996).

The group perspective relates to principles of *collaboration, common purpose, and controversy with civility*. The collaboration principle involves empowering others and self through trust. The common purpose principle refers to individuals working with shared aims and values. It implies the capacity to engage in a collective analysis of the issues at hand and the necessary tasks to be undertaken. The controversy with civility principle acknowledges two fundamental realities of any group effort, that differences in viewpoint are inevitable and valuable, and that these differences must be aired openly but with civility (HERI, 1996).

The final perspective is the *community/society* perspective. The citizenship principle describes the process where the individual is responsibly connected to the environment and the community. The interdependence of all involved in the leadership effort is acknowledged. Citizenship recognizes that effective democracy includes individual responsibility a well as individual rights (HERI, 1996).

The Social Change Model is presented as three circles connected by reciprocal arrows illustrating how the three clusters of values interact with and influenced each of the other principles. For example, the congruence principle (an individual perspective), affects and interacts with the common purpose principle (a group perspective), which ultimately affects citizenship (Astin, 1996; HERI, 1996). In this way, leadership development is integrative, multidimensional, and an ever-evolving process.

This model of leadership development is particularly useful to higher education professionals who are interested in preparing students for civic and community life. They should strive to meet students' needs with special attention given to the student's values. For example, if educators carefully observe the level of empathy, competence, patience, and self-awareness a student displays, they can help ensure that students are developing their leadership skills appropriately (Astin & Astin, 2000).

Over time, several authors have noted that there is a paucity of evidence in the literature that clearly defines leadership as an outcome of college experiences (Bowen, 1977; Pascarella & Terenzini, 2005). Instead, most research examines the frequency of student participation in leadership activities. But, participation may be a weak proxy for leadership development.

It is clear that an important goal for educators and program leaders is to empower students to become effective leaders and social change agents in society. To do this, they must first identify relevant indicators of leadership development and establish strategies for teaching students in such a way as to enhance leadership skills and competencies. The following sections provide a list of relevant variables related to leadership development and provide useful examples of how to approach learning assessment using various methods of inquiry.

## C. Relevant Variables

- serves as a role model
- is self awareness
- commits to civic responsibility
- initiates change for the common good
- collaborates with others
- builds trust
- sets goals/vision
- engages in teamwork
- resolves skills
- take risks
- offers leadership roles to others
- listens
- respects the dignity of others
- communicates directly and honestly
- mentors others

This list of variables is by no means an exhaustive list of all of the relevant variables associated with leadership development. Rather, it is intended to provide a point of departure for thinking about assessing the dimensions of learning related to leadership and leadership development.

As it is imperative to identify variables early in the assessment process, this list provides the reader with several variables that might be used. In general, the criterion (or dependent) variable essentially answers the question: What am I measuring? The predictor (or independent) variables, on the other hand, are those factors that are controlled or manipulated rather than observed. The predictor variable is often a grouping variable (for example, male versus female) and is the factor that is thought to be causal. For example, in most cases the dependent variable might be "leadership development" while "ability to set goals" may be one of the independent variables.

Recent research has proposed a grounded theory of how leadership identity develops (Komives, Owen, Longerbeam, Mainella, & Osteen, 2005) identifying a six stage model through which the student moves from a view of leadership as the behavior only of the positional leader to viewing leadership as a process among interdependent group members. This work expands Wielkiewicz's (2000) findings of two orthogonal factors of hierarchical or systemic views and illustrates that a student experiences leadership as hierarchical before moving to a systems view. This recent research has application for designing developmentally focused leadership programs.

Three major research studies are now underway to address leadership outcomes. The National Clearinghouse for Leadership Programs (NCLP) is conducting a study of leadership outcomes at 55 diverse institutions using the Social Change Model theoretical frame and Astin's IEO model design. A national and longitudinal study, the Wabash Study of Liberal Arts Education, is examining such outcomes as Effective Reasoning and Problem Solving, Inclination to Inquire and Lifelong Learning, Integration of Learning, Intercultural Effectiveness, Leadership, Moral Character, and Well-being. The Socially Responsible Leadership Scale-Revised is used as the leadership outcome measure in both of those studies. Concurrently, StudentVoice is developing an assessment measure of leadership outcomes. Readers are encouraged to seek the most recent publications of these three projects.

## D. Assessment Examples

Lee Durship is the Assistant Director for Student Activities at East Coast University. In this role, he is responsible for many programs including a leadership development program called, "Leaders Affecting Broader Society" (LABS). He and his colleagues have decided to assess the effectiveness of the program on developing students' leadership skills. Being a role model, setting goals/vision, and developing leadership in others were the independent variables that the team decided to use. In this regard, the team considered the following approaches:

1. Quantitative: To test the hypothesis that students participating in the leadership development program would demonstrate higher levels of leadership development skills and traits, Lee and his colleagues administered the self- and other- Student Leadership Practices Inventory (LPI) (Kouzes & Posner, 1998) to two groups. Using both versions of the LPI allowed for a 360 degree assessment rather than only a self-assessment. The control group consisted of randomly selected students who did not participate in the leadership development program. The experimental group consisted of those students participating regularly in the program. Data were analyzed using one-way ANOVA on each variable of interest, such as "inspiring a shared vision" to test for significant differences between the control and experimental groups.

2. Qualitative: To assess the impact of this program on students' leadership development, Lee and his colleagues decided to use phenomenology as a methodology to gain insight into students' lived experience as leaders. They asked each student to record in a journal their experiences and feelings that they believe were most critical to the success of their endeavors. In tape recorded interview sessions, the same students were interviewed individually about specific statements noted in their journals. During the interview, students were asked to expound upon their comments and to clarify any ambiguities. For example, if a student said, "I was successful due to my ability to work collaboratively," the interviewer asked the student to talk about

when, where, and how. After the interviews, the tapes were transcribed and Lee and his colleagues analyzed the transcripts searching for common themes then offered interpretations of these themes.

## E. Available Instruments

A word of caution—be certain that these instruments yield the type of data that you need to assess your program's effectiveness. To do this, first determine what you want to know and then search for the instrument that will provide you with such information. Do not do the reverse. If none of these instruments yield the kind of data that you are interested in, you are advised to develop your own instrument to meet your needs.

*Student Leadership Practices Inventory (Student LPI)*, by James M. Kouzes and Barry Z. Posner, 1995.
- Identifies specific behaviors and actions that enable college students to measure their own leadership capabilities; 30 items.
- Publisher: Jossey-Bass, A Wiley Company, 989 Market Street, San Francisco, CA 94103
- For more information: www.josseybass.com/WileyCDA/WileyTitle/productCd-0787944890.html

*Alleman Leadership Development Questionnaire (ALDQ)*, by Elizabeth Alleman, 1987.
- Measures mentoring activity between individuals in an organization or work unit.
- Publisher: Silverwood Enterprises, LLC, P.O. Box 363, Sharon Center, OH 44273; Telephone: 330-239-1646; FAX: 330-239-0250
- For more information: E-mail: silverasoc@aol.com

*Campbell Leadership Index*, by David Campbell, 1991.
- An adjective checklist designed to be used in the assessment of leadership characteristics Publisher: Pearson Reid London House, One North Dearborn, Suite 1600, Chicago, IL 60602
- For more information: www.pearsonreidlondonhouse.com/assessments/cli.htm

*College Student Experiences Questionnaire (CSEQ)*, by C. Robert Pace, 1994.
- Assesses the quality of effort students expend in using the resources and opportunities provided by the institution for their learning and development.
- Publisher: Center for Postsecondary Research and Planning Wright Education Bldg., rm. 4228 201 North Rose Avenue, Indiana University, Bloomington, IN 47405-1006, (812) 856-8041 (812) 856-8394 (fax)
- For more information: http://www.indiana.edu/~cseq/

*Leadership Appraisal Survey*, by Jay Hall, 1978.
- Assessment of one's leadership practices and attitudes by others.
- Publisher: Teleometrics International, 4567 Lake Shore Drive, Waco, TX 76710.
- For more information: www.teleometrics.com

*Leadership Skills Inventory (LSI)*, by Frances A. Karnes and Jane C. Chauvin, 1989.
- Measures strengths and weaknesses in leadership.
- Publisher: PRO-ED, 8700 Shoal Creek Blvd., Austin, TX 78757-6897.
- For more information: www.proedinc.com

*Socially Responsible Leadership Scale (SRLS)* by Tracy Tyree, 1997.
- This 114 items instrument measures the Social Change Model of Leadership and the 8 Cs (consciousness of self, congruence, commitment, common purpose, controversy with civility, collaboration, citizenship, and change). A revised version of the SRLS-R (Appel-Silbaugh, 2004), an 85 item version of the instrument, is also available.
- Publisher: National Clearinghouse for Leadership Programs, 0110 Stamp Student Union, the University of Maryland, College Park, MD 20742.
- For more information: www.nclp.umd.edu

Several purpose statements were adapted from those produced by the Buros Institute of Mental Measurements Test Reviews Online, www.unl.edu/buros.

## F. Related websites

| | |
|---|---|
| National Clearinghouse for Leadership Programs | http://www.nclp.umd.edu |
| International Leadership Association | http://www.academy.umd.edu/ila/ |
| Wabash Study of Liberal Arts Outcomes | http://www.liberalarts.wabash.edu/cila/nationalstudy |
| Evaluating Outcomes and Impacts | http://www.wkkf.org/Pubs/CCT/Leadership/Pub3780.pdf |
| Student Leadership and Higher Education | http://asstudents.unco.edu/students/AE-Extra/2001/2/Student.html |
| Leadership Library | http://www.asu.edu/mu/slp/library.htm |
| Greenleaf Center for Servant-Leadership | http://greenleaf.org/index.html |
| Leadership Online | http://www.leadershiponlinewkkf.org/ |

## G. References

Allen, K. E. & Cherry, C. (2000). Systematic leadership. Washington, DC: American College Personnel Association.

Astin, A. (1993). *What matters in college?* San Francisco: Jossey-Bass.

Astin, A. & Astin, H. (1996). A Social Change Model of Leadership Development (Guidebook III). Los Angeles: University of California, Higher Education Research Institute.

Astin, H. S. (1996). Leadership for social change. *About Campus*, 1(3), 4-10.

Astin, A. W. & Astin, H. S., (2000). Leadership reconsidered: Engaging higher education in social change. Battle Creek, MI: W. K. Kellogg Foundation.

Bennett, S. M., & Shayner, J. A. (1988). The role of senior administrators in women's leadership development. *New Directions for Student Services*, 44, 27-38.

Boccia, J. A. (1997). Introduction: The challenge of student leadership. *New Directions for School Leadership*, 4, 1-8.

Bowen, H. R. (1977). Investment in learning: *The individual and social value of American higher education*. San Francisco: Jossey-Bass.

Burns, J. M. (1978). *Leadership*. New York: Harper & Row.

Higher Education Research Institute. (1996). A social change model of leadership development (3rd ed.). Los Angeles: Author.

Komives, S., Lucas, N., & McMahon, T. (1998). *Exploring leadership: For college students who want to make a difference*. San Francisco: Jossey-Bass.

Komives, S. R., Owen, J. E., Longerbeam, S., Mainella, F. C., & Osteen, L. (2005). Developing a leadership identity: A grounded theory. *Journal of College Student Development*, 46, 593-611.

Lucas, C. J. (1994). *American higher education: A history*. New York: St. Martin's Griffin.

Morgan, A. E. (1960). Developing community responsibility. In W. D. Weatherford, Jr., (Ed.), *The goals of higher education*. Cambridge, MA: Harvard University Press.

Pascarella, E. T., & Terenzini, P. T. (2005). *How college affects students: A third decade of research*. San Francisco: Jossey-Bass.

Rogers, J. (2003). Leadership. In S. R. Komives, & D. B. Woodard, Jr. (Eds.) *Student Services: A handbook for the profession* (pp. 447-506). San Francisco: Jossey-Bass.

Wielkiewicz, R. M. (2000). The Leadership Attitudes and Beliefs Scale: An instrument for evaluating college students, thinking about leadership and organizations. *Journal of College Student Development*, 41, 335-347.

## H. Recommended Reading

Boatman, S. A. (1999). The leadership audit: A process to enhance the development of student leadership. *NASPA Journal*, 37, 325-336.

Brown, L., & Posner, B. (2001). Exploring the relationship between learning and leadership. *The Leadership & Organization Development Journal*, 22, 274-280.

Cassel, R. N. & Heichberger, R. L. (1975). *Leadership development: Theory and practice*. North Quincy, MA: Christopher Publishing House.

Connaughton, S. L., Lawrence, F. L., & Ruben, B. D. (2003). Leadership development as a systematic and multidisciplinary enterprise, *Journal of Education for Business*, 79, 46-51.

Cronin, T. E. (1995). Leadership and democracy. In J. Thomas Wren (Ed.), *The Leader's Companion*. New York: The Free Press.

Gardner, J. (1990). *On leadership*. New York: The Free Press.

Greenleaf, R. K. (1996). *On becoming a servant leader*. San Francisco: Jossey-Bass.

Greenleaf. R. D. (1973). *The servant as leader*. Revised Ed. Newton Center, MA: Robert K. Greenleaf Center.

Owen, J. E. (2001). An examination of leadership assessment. *Leadership Insights and Applications Series #11*. College Park, MD: National Clearinghouse for Leadership Programs.

Outcalt, C. L., Faris, S. K., & McMahon, K. N. (Eds.). (2000). *Developing non-hierarchical leadership on campus: Case studies and best practices in higher education*. Westport, CT: Greenwood Press.

Reinelt, C., Foster, P. & Sullivan, S. (2002). *Evaluating outcomes and impacts: A scan of 55 leadership development programs*. Brookline, MA: W. K. Kellogg Foundation.

van Linden, J. A. & Fertman, C. I. (1998). *Youth leadership: A guide to understanding leadership development in adolescents*. San Francisco: Jossey-Bass.

Zimmerman-Oster, K., & Burkhardt, J. C. (1999a). Leadership in the making: A comprehensive examination of the impact of leadership development programs on students. *The Journal of Leadership Studies*, 6, 50-66.

Zimmerman-Oster, K., & Burkhardt, J. C. (1999b). *Leadership in the making: Impact and insights from leadership development programs in U.S. colleges and universities*. Battle Creek, MI: W. K. Kellogg Foundation.

# Satisfying and Productive Lifestyles

"I am bored with it all."
—Winston Churchill

## A. Introduction

The causal relationship between formal education and various measures of well-being and satisfaction with life are complex (Pascarella & Terenzini, 1991; 2005). Some studies suggest that educational attainment has a positive direct effect on well-being and overall happiness, albeit small and statistically non-significant (Pascarella & Terenzini, 1991; 2005). Other studies indicate that formal education has a positive net influence on "dimensions of life that, in turn, increase one's sense of life satisfaction or overall happiness" (Pascarella & Terenzini, 2005, p. 553). Thus, although educational attainment seems to have a small and inconsistent impact on global well-being measures, education appears to have significant indirect effects on well-being and satisfaction by way of its influence on one's lifetime earnings, locus of control, and perceived health status (Ross & Wu, 1995).

Despite the fact that the relationship between education and satisfaction with life is tenuous, there is little question about the importance of life satisfaction to adult learners. Nearly all adults prize "self-fulfillment," happiness, or satisfaction with life as their most highly ranked goal (Heath, 1991). And, most Millenials hail life satisfaction as true success (Howe & Strauss, 2000). But, what is success? Douglas Heath (1991), professor emeritus of psychology at Haverford College, responded to this question: "Success isn't just a matter of luck, family privilege, or society's program; it has become more a matter of our character and the way we use it, for example, learning how to be persons of integrity" (p. 6).

More over, what is a satisfying and productive lifestyle? How can we measure satisfaction with life? Most would agree that satisfaction implies attainment, fulfillment, and acceptance. So, to be satisfied with life is to have at first lived, to have lived in such a way that there are few if any major regrets, and to believe that one's life made a difference somewhere, somehow, to someone. In short, satisfied lives are fulfilled lives and reflect the polar opposite of Winston Churchill's words in the quote aforementioned.

Satisfying and productive lifestyles is one of the 16 learning domains identified by the Council for the Advancement of Standards in Higher Education (CAS). Indicators of achievement of student learning and development in this area include achieving a balance between education, work, and leisure time.

CAS, the author, and consulting editors advise all educators to be concerned about measuring growth and development in this important area. Satisfaction with life is an ultimate outcome of not only college but life in general.

## B. Theoretical Contexts for Learning and Development

Theoretically speaking, satisfaction with life should be an ultimate life goal for all persons. Success and fame are two common expressions of satisfaction and have become increasingly important to college students (Howe & Strauss, 2000). For example, Heath (1991) wrote about Jane Allen who embodied vocational success—left home at an early age, started her own sporting supplies distribution business, and now grosses over $1 million dollars a year. Heath concluded that successful men and women are "happier and more satisfied with their lives than less successful persons are" (p. 184).

Apart from the apparent evidences of success that are often transitory and meaningless such as owning a big home or driving a fancy car, there are other indicators of success that are difficult to measure: happiness, peace, and satisfaction. Regardless of how its measured, the roots of one's satisfaction with life go far back into childhood and adolescence (Heath, 1991).

In that way, satisfying and productive lifestyles refers to an element of lifespan theory. Erikson (1959/1980, 1963, 1968) was the first psychologist to suggest a lifespan framework for identity development. Related to the work of Lewin (1936), Erikson described eight stages associated with identity development that are characterized by a central developmental crisis. Each crisis must be resolved successfully by balancing self and one's environment. His theory can be summarized as a conflict between trust and mistrust (Stage 1) to a crisis between integrity and despair (Stage 8). Stage 8 is based on "a need…to affirm one's existence and the meaning of one's life" (Evans, Forney, & Guido-DiBrito, 1998, p. 56). Successful resolution of all eight stages results in satisfaction.

Chickering (1969) provided a conceptual framework for identity development for college students. His theory is marked by seven vectors of development that contribute to the formation of identity. Though not rigidly sequential, Chickering's vectors were proposed to build on each other, leading to higher forms of complexity and integration at later stages. It is also important to note that students often find themselves revisiting issues associated with vectors they had previously resolved (Chickering & Reisser, 1993). The seven vectors of identity formation are: developing competence, managing emotions, moving through autonomy toward interdependence, developing mature interpersonal relationships, establishing identity, developing purpose, and developing identity. Vector seven, in particular, consists of developmental tasks closely related to this domain including developing clear vocational goals and making meaningful commitments.

Developmental theory is a useful tool for understanding learning and development of college students. Lifespan theories such as the one put forth by Erikson (1950) are particularly useful when examining life-long developmental processes like identify formation and satisfaction with life. Theories akin to Chickering's seven vectors provide a framework for operationalizing developmental constructs such as purpose. Therefore, all educators are strongly encouraged to consider how they might use theory as a tool for practice and vice versa.

## C. Relevant Variables

- achieves balance between education, work, and leisure time
- overcomes obstacles that hamper goal achievement
- articulates long-term goals and objectives
- manages interpersonal relationships
- is concerned for others
- uses creativity and imagination
- formulates ethics and behaves according to ethics
- forgives

- is resilient
- articulates and meets goals for work
- functions on the basis of personal, identity, ethical, spiritual, and moral values
- is committed to hard work
- is competent
- gives to others
- possess confidence
- succeeds
- deals with stress effectively
- possesses Integrity

This list of variables is by no means an exhaustive list of all of the relevant variables associated with satisfying and productive lifestyles. Rather, it is intended to provide a point of departure for thinking about assessing the dimensions of learning related to satisfying and productive lifestyles.

As it is imperative to identify variables early in the assessment process, this list provides the reader with several variables that might be used. As a general rule, the criterion (or dependent) variable essentially answers the question: What am I measuring? The predictor (or independent) variables, on the other hand, are those factors that are controlled or manipulated rather than observed. The predictor variable is often a grouping variable (for example, gender or year in college) and is the factor that is thought to be causal. For example, in most cases the dependent variable is the learning outcome while "generativity or giving back" may be one of the independent variables.

## D. Assessment Examples

Dr. Harry Life is Vice President for Student Affairs at Rising Falls College. He just finished re-reading Douglas Heath's *Fulfilling Lives* (1991). In the book, Heath summarized the results of his longitudinal study on the key contributors to happiness and success in adult life. Heath's study suggested that education contributes greatly to one's success and overall satisfaction with life. This raises an interesting question in Dr. Life's mind: What is the effect of college on students' satisfaction with life?

To investigate this question, he decided to use this theme in his first-year seminar section. He called his seminar "Satisfying Lives and College's Effects on Students." The course was limited to no more than 12. At the first class meeting, Dr. Life explained that the course is designed to give students hands-on research experience as they will work together to investigate one central research question: What is the effect of college on students' satisfaction with life?

After several weeks of instruction the team considered the following approaches:

1. Quantitative: First, they decided to create their own research instrument to gather information on specific variables such as dealing with stress, confidence, and generativity. All agreed that satisfaction with life was their dependent variable, but they needed to operationalize it so as to measure it meaningfully. Success and happiness were chosen as proxies for satisfaction. One question on their survey asked respondents to rank their level of personal success on a scale of 1 (least successful) to 7 (most successful). Another question asked participants to indicate their level of overall happiness using a similar scale. Other items on the survey asked the degree to which respondents felt education impacted their: ability to deal with stress, to gain confidence in self and others, and to give to others. The last section gathered demographic information including year in school, race, age, and gender. All responses were recorded in an electronic database.

   Responses were sorted into two groups—those who had less than one year of college experience and those who had at least one or more years of college. Using this information, the class created a dichotomous variable called "year in school" to indicate those who had less than one year and those who had one or more years of college. Demographic characteristics of the two groups were compared using Chi-Square tests. Differences in satisfaction with life were analyzed using multiple analyses of variance (MANOVA) tests on the various subscales with "year in school" as the independent variable. The results may suggest that those with more years of college report a statistically, significantly higher level of satisfaction with life than those with little or no college. The results might provide initial evidence of the effect of college on satisfaction with life.

2. Qualitative: To explore the effect of college on satisfaction with life using qualitative methods, the researchers decided to use a grounded theory methodology with focus group interviewing as the primary method of data collection. Focus groups are a form of group interviewing.

To do this, the student researchers invited "successful" students at Rising Falls College to participate in their study. These students were identified by the class, nominated by faculty members or administrators, or recently received recognition for an outstanding achievement. Fifteen "successful student leaders" were identified and recruited for this study. The class established an interview protocol to guide the focus group session and piloted the protocol on a random sample of average students.

The protocol was deemed appropriate by an advisory group of auditors so the researchers proceeded. The team conducted two focus group sessions and each session was limited to 90 minutes. Both sessions were tape-recorded and the class maintained their own field notes about the process and outcome of each session. Participants were asked to respond to the following prompts: How would you describe yourself in relationship to success? What contributes to this? How would you describe yourself in relationship to satisfaction? What contributes to this?

All audio tapes were transcribed by a professional. Transcripts were analyzed using the constant comparative method (Glaser & Strauss, 1967). That is, the researchers analyzed the data after the first session to consider more appropriate questions for the next session. Then, they reduced the data to individual units or "chunks of meaning" (Stage, 1992). Once all data were analyzed, they coded units by categorizing the data. The results provided a rich picture of the effect of college on satisfaction with life and overall happiness and success of these participants.

## E. Available Instruments

A word of caution—be certain that these instruments yield the type of data that you need to assess your program's effectiveness. To do this, first determine what you want to know and then search for the instrument that will provide you with such information. Do not do the reverse. If none of these instruments yield the kind of data that you are interested in, you are advised to develop your own instrument to meet your specific needs.

*Adaptive Behavior Assessment* by Patti L. Harrison and Thomas Oakland, n.d.
- A norm-referenced assessment of adaptive skills, second edition.
- Publisher: PsychCorp, 19500 Bulverde Road, San Antonio, TX 78259, customer_care@harcourt.com.
- For more information: www.PsychCorp.com and www.unl.edu/buros

*Health and Daily Living Form* by Rudolf H. Moos, Ruth C. Cronkite, and John W. Finney, n.d.
- Examines the resources and coping strategies used to prevent and adjust to stressful situations in life.
- Publisher: Mind Garden, Inc., 1690 Woodside Road, Suite #202, Redwood City, CA 94061, info@mindgarden.com.
- For more information: www.mindgarden.com

*Salubrious Lifestyle Scale from the Student Developmental Task and Lifestyle Assessment (SDTLA)* by Winston, Miller, & Cooper (1997), n.d.
- Measures via self-report the degree to which students exhibit health-related behavior, attitudes, and feelings and indicates degrees to which students adhere to a healthy lifestyle.
- Publisher: Student Development Associates, Inc. and is available from Appalachian State University.
- For more information: http://sdtla.appstate.edu/

*Computerized Lifestyle Assessment (CLA)* by Harvey A. Skinner, n.d.
- Designed to identify lifestyle behaviors such as health maintenance and emotional well-being.
- Publisher: Multi-health Systems, Inc., PO Box 950, North Tonawanda, NY 14120
- For more information: www.mhs.com

*Super's Work Values Inventory-Revised (WVI-R)* by Donald E. Super and Donald G. Zytowski, n.d.
- Measures relative importance of selected attributes of work.
- Publisher: National Career Assessment Services, Inc., 601 Visions Parkway, P.O. Box 277, Adel, IA 50003.
- For more information: www.ncasi.com or www.kuder.com

Several purpose statements were adapted from those produced by the Buros Institute of Mental Measurements Test Reviews Online, www.unl.edu/buros.

## F. Related Websites

| | |
|---|---|
| Journal of College and Character | www.collegevalues.org |
| Secret to a More Satisfying Life | http://www.true.com/magazine/psych_satisfyinglife.htm |
| Steps to a Satisfying Life | http://www.mnsu.edu/counseling/studentseightsteps.html |
| Creating a Satisfying Life | http://californiadivorce.info/ dm.psychology.next.satisfyinglife.htm |
| Character Strengths | http://halife.com/halife/character_strengths.html |

## G. References

Chickering, A. W. (1969). *Education and identity.* San Francisco: Jossey-Bass.

Chickering, A. W., & Reisser, L. (1993). *Education and identity* (2nd ed.). San Francisco: Jossey-Bass.

Erikson, E. H. (1950). *Childhood and society.* New York: Norton.

Erikson, E. H. (1963). *Childhood and society* (2nd ed.). New York: Norton.

Erikson, E. H. (1968). *Identity: Youth and crisis.* New York: Norton.

Erikson, E. H. (1980). *Identity and the life cycle.* New York: Norton. (Original work published 1959)

Evans, N. J., Forney, D. S., & Guido-DiBrito, F. (1998). *Student development in college: Theory, research, and practice.* San Francisco: Jossey-Bass.

Glaser, B. B., & Strauss, A. L. (1967). *The discovery of grounded theory. Strategies for qualitative research.* Hawthorne, NY: Aldine de Gruyter.

Heath, D. H. (1991). *Fulfilling lives: Paths to maturity and success.* San Francisco: Jossey-Bass.

Howe, N., & Strauss, W. (2000). *Millenials rising: The next great generation.* New York: Vintage Books.

Lewin, K. (1936). *Principles of typological psychology.* New York: McGraw-Hill.

Pascarella, E. T., & Terenzini, P. T. (2005). *How college affects students: A third decade of research.* San Francisco: Jossey-Bass.

Pascarella, E. T., & Terenzini, P. T. (1991). *How college affects students: Findings and insights from twenty years of research.* San Francisco: Jossey-Bass.

Ross, C., & Wu, C. L. (1995). The links between education and health. *American Sociological Review, 60,* 719-745.

Stage, F. K. (Ed.). (1992). *Diverse methods for research and assessment of college students.* Washington, DC: American College Personnel Association.

## H. Recommended Reading

Reid-Merritt, P. (2002). *Sister wisdom: 7 pathways to a satisfying life for soulful Black women.* San Francisco: Jossey-Bass.

Retton, Mary L. (2000). *Mary Lou Retton's Gateways to Happiness: 7 ways to a more peaceful, more prosperous, more satisfying life.* New York: Broadway.

# Meaningful Interpersonal Relationships

## A. Introduction

Martin Luther King, Jr., one of the most famous civil rights leaders in America, once said, "We must learn to live together as brothers [and sisters] or perish together as fools." The question arises—how do we learn to live together? And what is meant by "living together"—mere coexistence? Fundamentally, the essence of living together deals with relationship. That is, how one relates to another and how one interacts with all.

Meaningful interpersonal relationships is one of the learning domains identified by the Council for the Advancement of Standards in Higher Education (CAS). It is closely related to the issues of interconnectedness and mutuality. Achievement indicators range from connecting with and listening to others' points of view to treating others with respect and dignity.

College is not limited to an academic learning experience, but it is also a *living* experience as well. College students learn through a myriad of interactions with students, faculty, administrators, and environments. From these experiences, meaningful interpersonal relationships can form. In fact, many students report that they establish life-long friendships and love relationships during college. As educators, this learning outcome should be a priority alongside other outcomes such as developing critical thinking and leadership skills.

## B. Theoretical Contexts for Learning and Development

Theoretically speaking, this domain is related to psychosocial outcomes such as identity, intimacy, maturity, and trust. Erikson (1950, 1959) proposed a theory of the life cycle consisting of eight stages. Each stage is associated with certain ages ranging from infancy (0-1) to old age (65+). At each stage an individual is faced with a developmental crisis. Crisis, here, simply means that two polarities exist and the tension between them represents a crisis. Successful resolution of the conflict between the two polarities results in ideal accomplishments. For example, the sixth stage of Erikson's lifespan developmental model, intimacy and solidarity versus isolation, is the focus of psychosocial development during the college years. In this stage, two of the developmental accomplishments to be achieved are intimacy and love.

Since Erikson put forth his theory of the life cycle, a number of other models have emerged. Chickering (1969) proposed seven vectors of development that lead to establishing identity. His model outlines psychosocial development during the college years (Chickering & Reisser, 1993): developing competence, managing emotions, moving through autonomy toward interdependence, developing mature interpersonal relationships, establishing identity, developing purpose, and developing integrity. Chickering's model is not rigidly sequential and he noted that students tend to progress through these vectors at different rates. Vectors can interact with one another and students often revisit issues associated with vectors they had previously worked through and resolved.

Vectors three and four are closely related to this domain. During the third, students recognize the importance of their interconnectedness with others. Out of this awareness, students are able to develop mature interpersonal relationships. The tasks associated with vector four include "development of intercultural and interpersonal tolerance and appreciation of differences, as well as the capacity for healthy and lasting intimate relationships with partners and close friends" (Evans, Forney, & Guido-DiBrito, 1998, p. 39). Both tasks involve "the ability to accept individuals for who they are, to respect differences, and to appreciate commonalities" (Reisser, 1995, p. 509).

Loevinger, Wessler, and Redmore (1970) and Loevinger (1976) took a much more detailed approach and explained this process as ego development. Her model referred to that aspect of personality that assigns meaning to experiences. The term ego development thus refers to "a sequence...of interrelated patterns of cognitive, interpersonal, and ethical development that form unified, successive, and hierarchical world views" (Weathersby, 1981). Each worldview (or stage) represents a qualitatively different way of responding to or making meaning of life experiences. Loevinger's continuum of development describes the ego of being: impulsive, self-protective, conformist, conscientious-conformist, conscientious, individualistic, autonomous, and integrative. Each transition from a previous stage to the next represents an individual's restructuring of personality. The final stages are marked by the ability to respect others' individuality.

These theories lie at the core of education and reflect a few of the central aims of higher education. They are highly relevant to increased understanding of self, others, and self in relationship to others. In several ways, they relate to one's role as a citizen in a complex, global society. These theories are also central to an individuals' ability to learn from experience.

## C. Relevant Variables

- develops satisfying interpersonal relationships
- listens to others' point of view
- is civil and kind
- is dependable
- is able to work cooperatively with others by giving and taking
- has commitments
- establishes mutually rewarding relationships with friends
- treats others with respect
- trusts others
- assists others in need
- balances self-reliant behaviors with healthy forms of dependency
- is able to be intimate
- accepts others

This list of variables is by no means an all-inclusive list of the relevant variables associated with the development of meaningful interpersonal relationships. It is intended to provide a general starting point for thinking about assessing the effectiveness of educational programs relative to this domain. It is important to identify the dependent and independent variables early in the assessment process. The dependent variable essentially answers the question: What am I measuring? The independent variables are the factors that are controlled or vary, often referred to as a "treatment." For example, in most cases, the dependent variable may be "meaningful relationships" while "ability to work cooperatively" or "respect" may be one of the independent variables.

## D. Assessment Examples

Linda Hand is Coordinator of the Service-Learning Project at Hewlett University. In this position, she taught a service-learning course to undergraduates who lived in the student leadership community. The course had several objectives; one of which was to increase students' ability to establish meaningful interpersonal relationships. To assess the effectiveness of the class on students' interpersonal relationships, Linda decided to focus on three areas: understanding of self, respect for others, and interpersonal skills. She considered the following two approaches:

1. Quantitative: To measure the gains associated with the service-learning course, Linda adopted a test-retest design using three instruments: *Iowa Developing Autonomy Inventory* (Hood & Jackson, 1983), *Mines-Jensen Interpersonal Relationship Inventory* (Mines, 1977), and *Developing Purposes Inventory* (Barrett, 1978). The *Iowa Developing Autonomy Inventory* was used to measure understanding of self and emotional independence. It also provided information about the subscale, interdependence. The other two instruments were used to measure interpersonal skills (i.e., tolerance) and the quality of relationships, respectively. Linda administered the three instruments to all students in her class at the beginning of the semester and again at the end. Using the score from each inventory, Linda calculated gain scores for each of the three constructs (three scores) that she was interested in (i.e., respect for others). For example, she calculated a gain score on respect for others by subtracting the pretest score from the posttest score for each participant. This provided information about how individual students developed over the semester and may provide information about the effect of the class on students' interpersonal relationships.

2. Qualitative: Linda used a case study approach to measure learning in this domain. Case studies explore phenomena in a bounded system through interviews of a variety of people in the system, observations, and document review. "The case study is a frequently used approach to gathering qualitative information about a program" (Worthen, Sanders, & Fitzpatrick, 1997, p. 373). This is particularly useful in assessment and evaluation when the goal is to provide in-depth information about the single program rather than to generalize to "all programs" or a broader population (Guba & Lincoln, 1981; Stake, 1994). Throughout the semester, Linda assigned group projects and in-class assignments that students could work on in groups. The mid-term project required each pair to propose, organize, implement, and evaluate a service-learning project. For example, one pair decided to organize a relay-for-life event. They had to recruit participants, make flyers to publicize the event, collect money to donate to the cause, and oversee the actual day of the event. This required, but was not limited to teamwork, independence, respect, and trust. At the end of the semester, Linda asked students to respond in written form to the questions: What do you know about how you established your relationship with your partner? What was your role in the pair? How do you feel about that? She also conducted focus groups of students and service participants, and observed students in their service roles. To analyze data, Linda read through all interview responses and observation notes of what students *learned*. For example, she highlighted words like "trust" and phrases like "I can depend on her (him)" to explore differing perceptions on interpersonal relationships within the bounded system.

## E. Available Instruments

A word of caution—be certain that these instruments yield the types of data that are needed to assess the program's effectiveness. To do this, first determine what you want to know and then search for the instrument that will provide you with such information. Do not do the reverse. If none of these instruments yield the kind of data needed, you are strongly encouraged to create your own measurement tools to meet your needs.

*Assessment of Interpersonal Relations (AIR)* by Bruce A. Bracken, 1998.
- Developed to assess the quality of the relations young people have with important people in their lives.
- Publisher: Pro-ED, 8700 Shoal Creek Blvd., Austin, TX 78757-6897; proedrd2@aol.com
- For more information: www.proedinc.com; www.unl.edu/buros

*Developing Purposes Inventory* by Barrett, 1978.
- Designed to measure three subscales: avocational-recreational, vocational, and style of life; 45 items.
- Publisher: HITECH Press, PO Box 2341, Iowa City, IA 52242 or egbarra@befac.indstate.edu
- For more information: www.unl.edu/buros

*Intra- and Interpersonal Relations Scale (IIPS)* by G. G. Minnaar, n.d.
- Used to identify children's attitudes toward self and parents. Note: Though designed for use with children, it may be adapted for young adults.
- Publisher: Human Sciences Research Council, Private Bag X41, Pretoria, 0001, South Africa, NCWClassen@beauty.hsrc.ac.za
- For more information: www.unl.edu/buros

*Iowa Developing Autonomy Inventory* by Hood and Jackson, 1983.
- Used to measure six subscales: mobility, time management, money management, interdependence, and emotional independence; 90 items.
- Publisher: Al Hood, Counselor Education, The University of Iowa, Iowa City, IA 52242
- For more information: www.acpa.nche.edu/comms/comm09/dragon/

*Mines-Jensen Interpersonal Relationship Inventory* by Mines, 1977.
- Measures two subscales: tolerance and quality of relationships; 42 items.
- Publisher: No information available.
- For more information: www.unl.edu/buros

*Personal Assessment of Intimacy in Relationships (PAIR)* by David H. Olson and Mark T. Schaefer, 1992.
- Designed to measure the degree of intimacy in a relationship—both expected and realized intimacy.
- Publisher: Life Innovations, Inc., P.O. Box 190, Minneapolis, MN 55440-0190.
- For more information: www.unl.edu/buros

*Personal Relationship Inventory (PRI)* by Ronald L. Mann, 1995.
- Designed to measure one's capacity to love and engage in intimate interpersonal relationships.
- Publisher: Mann Consulting Group, 16070 Sunset Blvd. #105, Pacific Palisades, CA 90272.
- For more information: www.unl.edu/buros

*Student Developmental Task and Lifestyle Assessment.* R. B. Winston Jr., T. K. Miller, & D. L. Cooper 1997.
- The SDTA is designed to assess the development of college students and includes two developmental task scales associated with interpersonal relations. The Developing Autonomy Task (AUT). is defined by four subtasks: Emotional Autonomy, Interdependence, Academic Autonomy, and Instrumental Autonomy. Interdependence The Mature Interpersonal Relationships Task (MIR) is defined by two subtasks: Peer Relationships and Tolerance. The SDTLA is published by Student Development Associates, Inc. and is available from Appalachian State University. Order URL: http://sdtla.appstate.edu/

*Survey of Interpersonal Values (SIV)* by Leonard V. Gordon, 1978.
- Designed to assess certain values involving an individual's relationships with others.
- Publisher: Pearson Reid London House, One North Dearborn, Suite 1600, Chicago, IL 60602.
- For more information: http://www.pearsonreidlondonhouse.com/

Several purpose statements were adapted from those produced by the Buros Institute of Mental Measurements Test Reviews Online, www.unl.edu/buros.

## F. Related Websites

| | |
|---|---|
| "Deep listening" an important part of meaningful relationships | http://federalvoice.dscc.dla.mil/federalvoice/021106/boggs.html |
| Requirements of a meaningful relationship, healthy relationship | http://www.healthyplace.com/Communities/Relationships/serendipity/topics/topic078.htm |
| Meaningful relationships | http://www.irvingzola.com/rhips.htm |
| How to build trust | http://www.aish.com/family/marriage/How_To_Build_Trust_in_Marriage.asp |
| Trust | http://www.beyondintractability.org/m/trust_building.jsp |

## G. References

Barrett, W. R. (1978). *Construction and validation of the Developing Purposes Inventory*. Technical report. Iowa City: University of Iowa, Iowa Student Development Project.

Chickering, A. W. (1969). *Education and identity*. San Francisco: Jossey-Bass.

Chickering, A. W., & Reisser, L. (1993). *Education and identity* (2nd ed.). San Francisco: Jossey-Bass.

Erikson, E. H. (1950). *Childhood and society*. New York: Norton.

Erikson, E. H. (1959). *Identity and the life cycle*. Psychological Issues Monograph 1. New York: International Universities Press.

Evans, N. J., Forney, D. S., & Guido-DiBrito, F. (1998). *Student development in college: Theory, research, and practice*. San Francisco: Jossey-Bass.

Guba, E. G., & Lincoln, Y. S. (1981). *Effective evaluation*. San Francisco: Jossey-Bass.

Hood, A. B., & Jackson, L. M. (1983). *The Iowa Developing Autonomy Inventory*. Technical report. Iowa City: College of Education, University of Iowa.

Loevinger, J. (1976). *Ego development: Conceptions and theories*. San Francisco: Jossey-Bass.

Loevinger, J., Wessler, R., & Redmore, C. (1970). *Measuring ego development*. San Francisco: Jossey-Bass.

Mines, R. A. (1977). *Development and validation of the Mines-Jensen Interpersonal Relationships Inventory*. Technical report. Iowa City: University of Iowa, Student Development Project.

Reisser, L. (1995). Revisiting the seven vectors. *Journal of College Student Development*, 36, 505-511.

Stake, R. E. (1994). Case studies. In N. K. Denzin & Y. S. Lincoln (Eds.), *Handbook of qualitative research*. Thousand Oaks, CA: Sage.

Weathersby, R. P. (1981). Ego development. In A. W. Chickering & Associates (Eds.), *The modern American college: Responding to the new realities of diverse students and a changing society* (pp. 51-75). San Francisco: Jossey-Bass.

Worthen, B. R., Sanders, J. R., & Fitzpatrick, J. L. (1997). *Program evaluation: Alternative approaches and practical guidelines* (2nd ed.). White Plains, NY: Longman.

## H. Recommended Reading

Chirban, J. T. (2004). *True coming of age: A dynamic process that leads to emotional stability, spiritual growth, and meaningful relationships.* New York McGraw-Hill.

Duck, S. (1994). *Meaningful relationships: Talking, sense, and relating.* Thousand Oaks, CA: Sage.

Thatcher, B., Shadel, D. P., & Peck, M. S. (1997). *The power of acceptance: Building meaningful relationships in a judgmental world.* North Hollywood, CA: Newcastle Publishing.

Timmons, T., & Hedges, C. (1989). *Call it love or call it quits: The singles guide to meaningful relationships.* Cranbury, NJ: Worthy Publications.

# Realistic Self-Appraisal

## A. Introduction

Indicators of realistic self-appraisal include the ability to acknowledge and articulate personal skills and abilities as well as the ability to identify growth areas. Realistic self-appraisal implies capability to acknowledge one's own strengths and weaknesses. This domain of learning and development focuses on decisions made by an individual that are congruent with personal values and abilities. Ability to articulate a rationale for personal behavior, seeing value in feedback from others, and learning from past experiences are present and recognized in this domain.

Realistic self-appraisal indicates that an individual is capable of assessing personal strengths and weaknesses so further learning and development may occur (Sedlacek, 2004). Assessing self in relation to others without undue pressure from peer groups or authorities to alter judgment is evident when people apply realistic self-appraisal. Such individuals possess the ability to take corrective action when they perceive choices they have made will not allow them to accomplish their goals (Baxter Magolda, 1999).

## B. Theoretical Contexts for Learning and Development

This domain is related primarily to psychosocial development. Realistic self-appraisal is comprised of a clear sense of identity as well as a balanced intrapersonal foundation. As such, this domain is relevant to various aspects of the college experience. A clear sense of identity leads not only toward self-acceptance but also to acceptance of differences in others (Chickering, 1969; Erikson, 1968). A balanced intrapersonal foundation provides the basis for meaningful academic and social engagement (Baxter Magolda, 1999; Kegan, 1982).

Psychosocial theory provides insight into how the realistic self-appraisal construct is related to identity development (Baxter Magolda, 1999; Chickering & Reisser, 1993; Erikson, 1968). Sense of self is essential to clarified identity and to ego development and provides a psychosocial foundation for individual actions. Psychosocial developmental theory also acknowledges relationships with the external world that influence individual behavior. For example, Strange and Banning (2001) suggested that college environmental factors such as institutional size and curriculum exert powerful influence on student development in college.

Development in this domain is perceived as an increased ability to resolve issues associated with stage specific developmental crises. Successful resolution of these crises allows for individual development. During the college years, realistic self-appraisal implies that an individual has the ability to effectively resolve issues effectively associated with identity formation (Erikson, 1968).

Identity formation can be crucial for further development. "A solid sense of self" (Chickering, 1969, p. 80) allows an individual to form meaningful interpersonal relationships, a coherent sense of purpose, and a consistent set of beliefs and values (Chickering & Reisser, 1993).

Theories associate identity development with a set of shared personal and/or social characteristics. For example, recent theories have highlighted the differences in identity development among women and persons of color (Cross, 1971, 1978; Helms, 1990; Phinney, 1989; Torres, 1996). Others have explored identity development among gay, lesbian, and bisexual students (D'Augelli, 1991). Realistic self-appraisal may also be examined in regard to identity development among specific involvement groups such as student leaders and Greek letter organization members.

Realistic self-appraisal is also necessary for meaningful academic and social engagement. Development in this domain implies that an individual is operating from a coherent value and belief system. Individuals who know their own values and beliefs are able to engage in academic and social experiences that challenge them to identify and explore such issues (Baxter Magolda, 1999; Kegan, 1983).

Not only is sense of self essential to clarified identity, but sense of self in relation to others (intrapersonal awareness) is related to identity formation. For example, one's own belief system is formulated usually by carefully and critically analyzing views presented by others (Baxter Magolda, 1999). This has also been described as self-authorship (Baxter Magolda & King, 2004). This term describes the process an individual uses to reflect on their beliefs and organize personal thoughts in relation to those presented by others.

Realistic self-appraisal is a learning and development domain related to making meaning of the world and oneself and is therefore closely related to the academic and social success of students (Baxter Magolda, 1999).

## C. Relevant Variables

- sets realistic goals for self
- demonstrates self-authorship
- has accurate self-concept
- possess positive self-esteem
- articulates personal skills
- accepts differences
- demonstrates interdependence

- establishes locus of control
- demonstrates ability to make decisions
- identifies personal strengths
- identifies personal weaknesses
- acknowledges others' opinions of self
- accepts feedback from others

This list of variables is by no means an inclusive list of all of the relevant variables associated with self-appraisal. It is intended to provide a general starting point for thinking about assessing the effectiveness of a program relative to self-appraisal. It is important to identify the dependent and independent variables early in the assessment process. The dependent variable essentially answers the question: What am I measuring? The independent variables are the factors that are controlled or vary, often referred to as a "treatment." For example, in most cases, the dependent variable might be "self-appraisal" or some form of ability or skill. In other cases, self-appraisal may serve as an independent variable that is related to the dependent variable.

## D. Assessment Examples

Dr. Rhea List is the Director of Multicultural Programs at East Soho University (ESU), a large, comprehensive university in the northeastern region of the country. It enrolls a very diverse group of learners and many adult learners (e.g., non-traditionally aged). In her position, Rhea oversees the Adult Leaders of Tomorrow (ALOT) program. This program is designed to provide unique leadership learning opportunities to students from various cultural backgrounds. Students receive hands-on instruction and experience on leadership. To evaluate the effectiveness of her program, Dr. List coordinates a collaborative assessment team effort and considers the following approaches:

1. Quantitative: One of the program's objectives is for students to identify their own leadership style and to be able to evaluate their own leadership ability. Several aspects of the program are geared towards understanding one's self and identifying one's own strengths and weaknesses. To understand the relationship between sense of self and leadership ability, the team created their own instrument called "ALOT Research Tool" or ART for short. To design their instrument, they adapted items with permission from the *Developing the Leader Within (DLW)* survey published by Mind Garden and *Dimensions of Self-Concept* survey by Michael, Smith, and Michael (1992). The final survey consisted of 15 items. The dependent variable was "self-perceived leadership ability" and the independent variable included effective leadership and participation in ALOT. The latter was coded using "1" for ALOT respondents and "0" for non-ALOT respondents.

   The final survey was administered to all ALOT participants and a random selection of non-ALOT students at Eastern Soho University. The final sample included 230 participants; 100 ALOT participants and 130 non-ALOT students. Analysis of variance (ANOVA) was used to compare self-perceived leadership skills and effective leadership scores of the two groups to determine whether ALOT participants' perceptions of their leadership abilities were more realistic than those who did not participate.

2. Qualitative: As previously mentioned, one of the program's objectives is for students to identify their own leadership style and to be able to evaluate their own leadership ability. To explore the relationship between one's self-perception of his/her leadership ability and how others view the individual's leadership skills, the assessment team used case study (methodology) to collect data from ten student who participated in A LOT over the four to five years of their college experience. Each team member followed two students. Data were collected from a number of sources including papers/writing samples, extracurricular transcripts, academic transcripts, recommendation letters, evaluations, and job applications. A team constant comparative analysis approach was employed. That is, periodically, the team members met to discuss what they were learning from the students to which they were assigned. This enabled each member of the team to benefit from the other four colleagues' insights and perspectives. In addition, the team conducted exit interviews with each participant shortly before graduation from ESU. In the exit interviews, participants were asked to talk about their strengths, weaknesses, leadership skills, and academic abilities.

   "The case study is a frequently used approach to gathering qualitative information about a program" (Worthen, Sanders, & Fitzpatrick, 1997, p. 373). The emphasis of a case study is placed on the case itself and, in this instance, the ALOT program. This is particularly useful in assessment and evaluation when the goal is to provide in-depth information about the single program rather than to generalize to "all programs" or a broader population (Guba & Lincoln, 1981; Stake, 1994). The data provided useful information about participants' leadership experiences and abilities, their academic and extracurricular involvement, and feedback from others about their abilities and weaknesses. By gathering rich, thick data from 10 individuals and sharing their findings in a group setting, the assessment team is able to draw conclusions about the effectiveness of their program for those who participated in the program. In this way, the unit of analysis shifts from the individual to the programmatic case. This approach allows the team to explore the influence of ALOT on how realistic self-appraisal is influenced by leadership ability.

## E. Available Instruments

A word of caution—be certain that the instruments selected yield the type of data needed to assess the program's effectiveness. To do this, first determine what you want to know and then search for the instrument(s) that will provide such information. Do not do the reverse. If no instrument is found that will yield the kind of data desired, it is advisable to develop a tool to obtain the desired data.

*Dimensions of Self-Concept* by William B. Michael, Robert A. Smith, and Joan J. Michael, n.d.
- Measures non-cognitive factors associated with self-esteem or self-concept in an academic setting. The instrument consists of 80 items (Likert format) and measures five dimensions that are considered central to self-concept: (1) Level of Aspiration, (2) Anxiety, (3) Academic Interest and Satisfaction, (4) Leadership and Initiative, and (5) Identification Versus Alienation.
- Publisher: Educational & Industrial Testing Service (EdITS), (619) 222-1666
- For more information: www.unl.edu/buros

*Student Developmental Task & Lifestyle Assessment (SDTLA)*, by R. B. Winston, Jr., T. K. Miller, & D. L. Cooper, 1997.
- Measures personal development and growth of college students, Four forms: 1.99 = 153 items (3 Developmental Tasks + 2 Scales); 2.99 = 57 items (Establishing & Clarifying Purpose); 3.99 = 57 items (Developing Autonomy); 4.99 = 47 items (Developing Mature Personal Relationships).
- Publisher: Student Development Associates, Inc., Athens, GA, Available from Appalachian State University, Phone (828) 262-2060; e-mail <sdtla@appstate.edu>
- For more information: http://www.sdtla.appstate.edu

*Developing Purpose Inventory* by William R. Baratt and Albert B. Hood, n.d.
- The Developing Purpose Inventory is designed to measure the extent to which students view themselves as becoming more goal directed, independent, and focused on interests as a result of their higher-education experience. The Developing Purpose Inventory (Likert format) is comprised of three scales: (1) Avocational-Recreational Purpose, (2) Vocational Purpose, and (3) Style of Life.
- For more information: www.unl.edu/buros

*Personal Effectiveness Inventory (PEI)* by Human Synergistics International, n.d..
- Designed to provide information about personal attitudes, beliefs, and behavior to increase skills for effectiveness.
- Publisher: Human Synergistics International, 39819 Plymouth Road, C-8020, Plymouth, MI 48170-8020.
- For more information: www.humansyn.com

*Personal Inventory of Needs* by Training House, Inc.
- Self-assessment tool designed to identify personal strengths and needs.
- Publisher: Training House, Inc., 22 Amherst Road, Pelham, MA 01002-9745.
- For more information: www.unl.edu/buros

*Personal Style Indicator (PSI)* by Terry D. Anderson, Everett T. Robinson, Jonathan Clark, and Susan Clark, 1998.
- Designed to identify personal beliefs and interaction styles and to increase self-awareness.
- Publisher: Consulting Resource Group International, Inc., #386-200 West Third Street, Sumas, WA 98295-8000.
- For more information: www.unl.edu/buros

*Self-Perception Profile for College Students* by Jennifer Neeman and Susan Harter, 1992.
- Designed to measure students' self-concept.
- Publisher: Susan Harter, Ph.D., University of Denver, Department of Psychology, 2155 South Race Street, Denver, CO 80208-0204.
- For more information: www.unl.edu/buros; sharter@du.edu

Several purpose statements were adapted from those produced by the Buros Institute of Mental Measurements Test Reviews Online, www.unl.edu/buros.

## F. Related Websites

| | |
|---|---|
| Jung Typology Test | http://www.humanmetrics.com/cgi-win/JTypes1.htm |
| What's your personality style? | http://www.platinumrule.com/assessment.asp |
| Self-appraisal | http://www.columbia.edu/cu/ssw/careers/tips/self_appraisal.html |
| Self assessment worksheet | http://hsc.uwe.ac.uk/pec/Selfassessment.pdf |
| What are your greatest strengths and weaknesses? | http://interview.monster.com/articles/biggest/ |

## G. References

Baxter Magolda, M. (1999). *Creating contexts for learning and self-authorship: Constructive developmental pedagogy*. Nashville, TN: Vanderbilt University Press.

Baxter Magolda, M., & King, P. M. (2004). *Learning partnerships: Theory and models of practice to educate for self-authorship*. Sterling, VA: Stylus.

Chickering, A. W. (1969). *Education and identity*. San Francisco: Jossey-Bass.

Chickering, A. W., & Reisser, L. (1993). *Education and identity* (2nd ed.). San Francisco: Jossey-Bass.

Cross, W. E., Jr. (1971). Toward a psychology of black liberation: The negro-to-black conversion experience. *Black World*, 20(9), 13-27.

Cross, W. E., Jr. (1978). The Thomas and Cross models of psychological Nigrescence: A review. *Journal of Black Psychology*, 5, 13-31.

D'Augelli, A. R. (1991). Gay men in college: Identity processes and adaptations. *Journal of College Student Development*, 32, 140-146.

Erikson, E. H. (1968). *Identity: Youth and crisis*. New York: Norton.

Guba, E. G., & Lincoln, Y. S. (1981). *Effective evaluation*. San Francisco: Jossey-Bass.

Helms, J. E. (Ed.). (1990). *Black and white racial identity: Theory, research and practice*. Westport, CT: Praeger.

Kegan, R. (1982). *The evolving self*. Cambridge, MA: Harvard University Press.

Phinney, J. S. (1989). Stages of ethnic identity development in minority group adolescents. *Journal of Early Adolescence*, 9, 34-49.

Sedlacek, W. E. (2004). *Beyond the big test: Non-cognitive assessment in higher education.* San Francisco: Jossey-Bass.

Stake, R. E. (1994). Case studies. In N. K. Denzin & Y. S. Lincoln (Eds.), *Handbook of qualitative research.* Thousand Oaks, CA: Sage.

Strange, C. and Banning, J. (2001), *Education by design.* San Francisco: Jossey-Bass.

Torres, V. (1996). *Empirical studies in Latino/Latina ethnic identity.* Paper presented at the National Association of Student Personnel Administrators National Conference, Baltimore, MD.

Worthen, B. R., Sanders, J. R., & Fitzpatrick, J. L. (1997). *Program evaluation: Alternative approaches and practical guidelines* (2nd ed.). White Plains, NY: Longman.

## H. Recommended Reading

Baxter Magolda, M. (1999). *Creating contexts for learning and self-authorship: Constructive developmental pedagogy.* Nashville, TN: Vanderbilt University Press.

Buckingham, M., & Clifton, D. O. (2001). *Now, discover your strengths.* Princeton, NJ: Gallup.

Denzin, N. K., & Lincoln, Y. S. (Eds.). (1994). *Handbook of qualitative research.* Thousand Oaks, CA: Sage.

Douglas, J. D. (1985). *Creative interviewing.* Beverly Hills, CA: Sage.

Krueger, R. A. (1994). *Focus groups* (2nd ed.). Thousand Oaks, CA: Sage.

Lesli, M. (2002). *The magical personality: Identify strengths and weaknesses to improve your magic.* St. Paul, MN: Llewellyn Publications.

Patton, M. Q. (1987). *How to use qualitative methods in evaluation.* Newbury Park, CA: Sage.

Sedlacek, W.E. (2004). *Beyond the big test: Noncognitive assessment in higher education.* San Francisco: Jossey-Bass.

Tesch, R. (1990). *Qualitative research: Analysis types and software tools.* New York: Falmer Press.

Yin, R. K. (1984). *Case study research.* Beverly Hills, CA: Sage.

# Enhanced Self-Esteem

## A. Introduction

College students are challenged with balancing the demands of academics, developing new social contacts, and being responsible for their own every day needs. Making the transition to college creates a situation where regular contact with traditional support groups like family and friends can be reduced.

Various developmental issues and environmental conditions influence student development and identity. Having a good sense of self or self-concept is one of the most important influential factors.

One component of self-concept is self-esteem. A high level of self-esteem is key for a student's success. Self-esteem can be described as a positive or negative orientation toward oneself and an overall evaluation of one's value or worth. Having high self-esteem indicates positive self-regard rather than egotism as some theorists have suggested (Rosenberg, n.d.).

Enhanced self-esteem is one of the 16 student learning and development outcome domains identified by CAS. Indicators of self-esteem include showing self-respect and respect for others, initiating actions towards achievement of goals, taking reasonable risks, demonstrating assertive behaviors, and functioning without need for constant reassurance from others.

Self-esteem is a popular and widely researched topic particularly in psychology (Mecca, Smelser, & Vasconcellos, 1989). A major reason for its popularity is its pervasive impact on various facets of human behavior including achievement, performance, motivation and competition (Baumeister, 1993; Bednar, Wells, & Peterson, 1989; Campbell, 1990; Wells & Marwell, 1976; Wylie, 1974, 1979).

Mirowsky and Ross (1989) and Rosenberg (1989) noted that self-esteem is influenced by others' opinions and evaluations of one as a person of worth. Perceived self-worth comes from social attachments to close friends, family members, parents, and teachers and is a function of appraisals of these constituents (Rosenberg, 1979; 1989).

Students with low self-esteem seem to know less about themselves than students with high self-esteem (Baumgardner, 1990; Campbell, 1990). Their views about themselves change from day to day and they have fewer definite beliefs about what they are like and who they are as people than students with higher self-esteem (Baumeister, 1993). Developmentally, students with low self-esteem lack an important aspect of their identity with which they cope during the college years.

Within the college environment, the expectation is that all functional area programs will emphasize learning and identify relevant learning outcomes. Using CAS functional area standards and guidelines will allow program leaders to assess student achievement. The goal here is to help program leaders assess their programs' influence on student self-esteem.

## B. Theoretical Contexts for Learning and Development

One way to broaden our understanding of self-esteem as it relates to learning and development outcomes is to use theoretical models. Self-esteem results from others' evaluations of personal worth (Mirowsky & Ross, 1989) and has beneficial emotional consequences when present or like low levels of depression when not present (Pearlin, Menaghan, Lieberman, & Mullan, 1981).

The Establishing Identity vector, the fifth of Chickering's seven vectors in his Identity Development theory, includes self-esteem as a component. Flowers (2002) suggested that in this vector students are beginning to become aware of and learn to develop their own identity.

Students discover their core characteristics from challenge and support efforts provided in their environments including, classes and clubs, relationships, reflective moments, and revelations. Their comfort level with gender, sexual orientation, race, ethnicity, abilities, etc, including their preferred ways to dress and their favorite things to do, are all part of the establishing identity vector. Students make preliminary choices and commitments about the individuals with whom they identify, the roles they can play, and the lifestyles they want, and they get feedback from others that may confirm their self-image or transform it (Reisser, 1995). Some racial identity theorists noted that students of color begin identity development from a low esteem as mirrored by attitudes of the dominant culture. Experiences with role models from their own group encourage a stronger sense of self (Cross, 1971, 1978; Helms, 1990).

Whether self-esteem affects academic performance has been debated for some time. For example, some theorists suggested that high self-esteem improves academic achievement. But others argued that simply feeling good about oneself does little to achieve good test scores since one's effort is not increased. Others took this argument a step further and claimed that self-esteem contributes to slackened efforts among individuals because if they feel good about themselves, they have no incentive to strive to meet higher standards of accomplishment. These theorists believe that it is the effort associated with perceptions of control that leads to high self-esteem and academic success, rather than the good feelings about one-self (Hewitt, 1998).

Additionally, theorists have argued that self-esteem does affect academic performance and the consequences of self-esteem are real for a number of reasons. First, self-consistency theory states that self-esteem shapes behavior because of the self-consistency motive (Rosenberg, Schooler, & Schoenbach, 1989). People act in a manner that is consistent with their self-concept, so adolescents with high self-esteem are likely to get good grades (Ross & Broh, 2000).

Second, self-enhancement theory suggests that self-esteem affects academic performance because individuals with low self-esteem may reject standards such as doing well in school. If this behavior is repetitive, academic failure could be the result (Covington, 1984; Kaplan, 1980).

Last, self-esteem theory proposes that if a student feels that he or she is a good student, they are more likely to experience positive academic performance than if they simply feel that they are a good person (Marsh, 1993; Rosenberg, Schooler, Schoenbach, & Rosenberg, 1995).

Though the previous theoretical arguments for self-esteem's effect on academic performance suggest a correlation, they fail to explain the role that motivation, effort, and agency play in the process (Covington, 1984; Kaplan, 1980). However, any experience that helps students define who they are and who they are not, can help solidify self-esteem or a sense of self. Colleges and universities provide many opportunities for students to explore the various aspects of self and to understand how the interlocking aspects of the body, mind, feelings, beliefs, values, and priorities all constitute a coherent sense of self with a continuity of experience. The result is personal stability and integration (Reisser, 1995).

## C. Relevant Variables

- develops a self concept
- develops a sense of self
- establishes identity
- confirms self-image
- confirms self-worth
- shows self-respect

- demonstrates assertive behaviors
- acknowledges personal qualities
- feels useful
- feels proud of oneself
- demonstrates personal control
- takes reasonable risks

This list of variables is by no means an inclusive list of all of the relevant variables associated with the development of self-esteem. It is intended to provide a general starting point for thinking about assessing the effectiveness of a program aimed to enhance self-esteem. It is important to identify the dependent and independent variables early in the assessment process. The dependent variable essentially answers the question: What am I measuring? The independent variable are the factors that are controlled or vary, often referred to a "treatment." For example, in most cases, the dependent variable might be "self-esteem" while "showing self-respect" may be one of the independent variables.

## D. Assessment Examples

Dr. Seth Esteam is the Dean of Students at West Shore University. In this role, he is responsible for overseeing a program called "R-TEC." The acronym stands for "Returning to Excel in College." It is a program designed for college students who are returning to campus after being dismissed for a semester or two on academic probation. Students in this program are required to attend group meetings each week, to meet with their academic counselor regularly, and to participate in seminars and workshops scheduled throughout the semester. One of the main objectives of R-TEC is to increase a student's level of self-esteem so as to increase their confidence and ultimately their achievement in college. Recently, Dr. Esteam had lunch with a colleague who was interested in learning more about academic support programs like R-TEC. His colleague asked, "Does the program work? Do R-TEC students demonstrate increased self-esteem levels after participating in the program?" Dr. Esteam said, "Yes" with confidence though he had never collected data to support his answer. At the next staff meeting, Dr. Esteam announced that he was implementing a component of the program designed to assess its effectiveness on several learning outcomes—self-esteem being the first of them. To do this, he assigned his associate director, Ms. Mia Self, the task of managing the entire project. Ms. Self selected "academic ability," "relationship with others," "family acceptance," and "personal perceptions" as the main factors that are addressed in the program relative to self-esteem. These variables are also the subscales of the *Self Esteem Index (SEI)* by Brown and Alexander (1992).

1. Quantitative: Ms. Self and her colleagues used a pretest-posttest research design to evaluate the program. At the initial meeting, all 50 participants were assigned a random ID number and were asked to complete the *Self-Esteem Index (SEI)*. In addition, 50 non-R-TEC students were randomly selected and asked to complete the SEI. Responses were scored using the *SEI Manual and Profile* and all scores were entered into a database

as "Score1" using the random ID number to identify participants. R-TEC students were coded "1" on the variable "TECstatus" while non-R-TEC students were coded "0." At the end of the semester, all students were asked to complete the *Self-Esteem Index (SEI)* again using the same ID number. Responses were scored and entered into a database as "Score2." R-TEC and non-R-TEC students were coded as mentioned previously.

To analyze the data, Dr. Esteem conducted analysis of covariance (ANCOVA) tests using the "pretest" as a covariate. This is an appropriate use of the statistic since "a covariate is…nothing but an independent variable which, because of the logic dictated by the substantive issues of research, assumes priority among the set of independent variables as a basis for accounting for Y variance" (Cohen, 1968, p. 439). Intuitively, we know that differences in the post-test scores may be attributable to initial differences in the pre-test scores. In order to control the pre-existing differences, the effect of the covariate (pre-test) has to be removed from the post-test score. This will allow the team to evaluate whether there is a significant difference between the groups after removing the effects of initial differences measured by the pretest. The results will provide them with information about the effect of R-TEC on students' self-esteem.

2. Qualitative: To explore the effect of R-TEC on returning students' levels of self-esteem, Ms. Self and her colleagues posed the following research questions using a phenomenological approach: How do students in the program experience self-esteem? This question is best addressed by a qualitative methodology because it allows for the exploration of complex processes such as self-esteem. To this end, the team collected data from a number of sources. Students were asked to write a weekly 2-page response to the following questions: How do you feel about yourself as a student right now? What experiences have contributed to how you feel about yourself? To analyze the data, the team read and reread the responses and identified themes. As reading progressed new themes emerged. Eventually, the evaluators sought to uncover and interpret meaning of the themes. Deeper interpretation occurred by the writing and rewriting of the themes (van Manen, 1990). To ensure goodness of data, Ms. Self conducted member checks and convened a human science dialogue (Jones, Torres & Arminio, 2006).

## E. Available Instruments

A word of caution—be certain that these instruments yield the types of data needed to assess the program's effectiveness. To do this, first determine what you want to know and then search for the instrument that will provide you with such information. Do not do the reverse. If none of these instruments yields the kind of data in which you are interested, you are advised to develop your own measurement tools to meet your needs.

*Coopersmith Self-Esteem Inventory (SEI)*, (adult form), by Stanley Coopersmith, 1981.
- Measures attitudes toward self in social and personal contexts; 25 items.
- Publisher: Consulting Psychologists Press, 3803 East Bayshore Road, Palo Alto, CA 94303,
   Telephone: (800) 624-1765 or (415) 969-8608.
- For more information: http://wbarratt.indstate.edu/dragon/saroi/sa-sei.htm

*Multidimensional Self-Esteem Inventory (MSEI)*, by Edward J. O'Brien and Seymour Epstein, 2004.
- Measures global self-esteem and its eight components: Competence, lovability, likability, personal power, self-control, moral self-approval, body appearance, and body functioning; 116 items.
- Publisher: Psychological Assessment Resources, Inc., 16204 N. Florida Ave., Lutz, FL 33549,
   Telephone: (813) 968-3003.
- For more information: http://www.parinc.com/product.cfm?ProductID=239

*Rosenberg Self-Esteem Scale (RSE)*, Morris Rosenberg, 1965.
- To measure an individual's self-worth, 10 items.
- Publisher: The Morris Rosenberg Foundation, c/o Dept. of Sociology, University of Maryland, 2112 Art/Soc Building, College Park, MD 20742-1315.
- For more information: http://www.bsos.umd.edu/socy/grad/socpsy rosenberg.html

*Self-Esteem Index, (SEI)*, by Linda Brown and Jacquelyn Alexander, 1992.
- Measures the way individuals perceive themselves using a 4-point scale, 80 items.
- Publisher: PRO-ED, 8700 Shoal Creek Blvd., Austin, TX 78757-6897, Telephone: (800) 897-3202; FAX: (512) 451-8542; E-mail: proedrd2@aol.com;
- For more information: WWW.PROEDINC.COM

*Student Developmental Task & Lifestyle Assessment (SDTLA)*, by R. B. Winston, Jr., T. K. Miller, & D. L. Cooper, 1997.
- Measures personal development and growth of college students, Four forms: 1.99 = 153 items (3 Developmental Tasks + 2 Scales); 2.99 = 57 items (Establishing & Clarifying Purpose); 3.99 = 57 items (Developing Autonomy); 4.99 = 47 items (Developing Mature Personal Relationships).
- Publisher: Student Development Associates, Inc., Athens, GA, Available from Appalachian State University, Phone (828) 262-2060; e-mail sdtla@appstate.edu
- For more information: http://www.sdtla.appstate.edu

## F. Related Websites

| | |
|---|---|
| Self-esteem | www.macses.ucsf.edu/research/Psychosocial/notebook/selfesteem.html |
| Rosenberg Self-esteem Scale | www.bsos.umd.edu/socy/grad/socpsy rosenberg.html |
| More Self-esteem | www.more-selfesteem.com |
| National Association for Self-Esteem | www.self-esteem-nase.org |
| Mythoself | www.mythoself.com/character-coaching-and-computers/college-self-esteem-student.html |

## G. References

Baumgardner, A. H. (1990). To know oneself is to like oneself: Self-certainty and self-affect. *Journal of Personality and Social Psychology*, 58, 1062-1072.

Baumeister, R. F. (1993). Understanding the inner nature of low self-esteem: Uncertain, fragile, protective and conflicted. In R. F. Baumeister (Ed.), *Self-esteem: The puzzle of low self-regard*, (pp. 201-218). New York: Plenum Press.

Baumeister, R. F. (Ed.). (1993). *Self-esteem: The puzzle of low self-regard*. New York: Plenum Press.

Bednar, R. L., Wells, M. G., & Peterson, S. R. (1989). *Self-esteem: Paradoxes and innovations in clinical theory and practice*. Washington, D.C.: American Psychological Association.

Campbell, J. D. (1990). Self-esteem and clarity of the self-concept. *Journal of Personality and Social Psychology*, 59, 538-549.

Cohen, J. (1968). Multiple regression as a general data-analytic system. *Psychological Bulletin*, 70, 426-443.

Covington, M. (1984). The motive for self-worth. In R. A. Ames and C. Ames (Ed.), *Research on motivation in education* (pp. 77-113). New York: Academic Press.

Cross, W. E., Jr. (1971). Toward a psychology of black liberation: The negro-to-black conversion experience. *Black World*, 20(9), 13-27.

Cross, W. E., Jr. (1978). The Thomas and Cross models of psychological Nigrescence: A review. *Journal of Black Psychology*, 5, 13-31.

Flowers, L. (2002). Developing purpose in college: Differences between freshmen and seniors. *College Student Journal*, 36, 478-84.

Helms, J. E. (Ed.). (1990). *Black and white racial identity: Theory, research and practice*. Westport, CT: Praeger.

Hewitt, J. (1998). *The myth of self-esteem*. New York: St. Martin's Press.

Jones, S. R., Torres, V., & Arminio, J. (2006). *Negotiating the complexities of qualitative research*. New York: Brunner-Routledge.

Kaplan, H. (1980). *Deviant behavior in defense of self*. New York: Academic Press.

Marsh, H. W. (1993). Relations between global and specific domains of self: The importance of individual importance, certainty, and ideals. *Journal of Personality and Social Psychology*, 65, 975-992.

Mecca, A. M., Smelser, N. J., & Vasconcellos, J. (Eds.). (1989). *The social importance of self-esteem*. Berkeley: University of California Press.

Mirowsky, J. & Ross, C. E. (1989). *Social causes of psychological distress*. New York: Aldine de Gruyter.

Pearlin, L. I., Menaghan, E. G., Lieberman, M. A., & Mullan, J. T. (1981). The stress process. *Journal of Health and Social Behavior*, 22, 337-356.

Reisser, L. (1995). Revisiting the seven vectors. *Journal of College Student Development*, 36, 505-511.

Rosenberg, M. (1979). *Conceiving the self*. New York: Basic Books.

Rosenberg, M. (1989). *Society and the adolescent self-image*. Middletown, CT: Wesleyan University Press.

Rosenberg, M., Schooler, C., & Schoenbach, C. (1989). Self-esteem and adolescent problems: Modeling reciprocal effects. *American Sociological Review*, 54, 1004-1018.

Rosenberg, M., Schooler, C., & Schoenbach, C. & Rosenberg, F. (1995). Global self-esteem and specific self-esteem: Different concepts, different outcomes. *American Sociological Review*, 60, 141-156.

Ross, C. E. & Broh, B. A. (2000). The roles of self-esteem and the sense of personal control in the academic achievement process. *Sociology of Education*, 73, 270-284.

Rosenberg Self-Esteem Scale, (n.d.). Retrieved January 10, 2005 from http://www.bsos.umd.edu/socy/grad/socpsy roseberg.html

Van Manen, M. (1990). *Researching lived experience*. Albany: The State university of New York Press.

Wells, L. E. & Marwell, G. (1976). *Self-esteem*. Beverly Hills, CA: Sage.

Wylie, R. (1974). *The self-concept (Vol. 1)*. Lincoln: University of Nebraska Press.

Wylie, R. (1979). *The self-concept (Vol. 2)*. Lincoln: University of Nebraska Press.

## H. Recommended Reading

Astin, A. (1993). *What matters in college?* San Francisco: Jossey-Bass.

Chickering, A. W. (1969). *Education and identity*. San Francisco: Jossey-Bass.

Chickering, A. W. & Reisser, L. (1993). Education and identity (2nd ed.). San Francisco: Jossey-Bass.

Mone, M. A., Baker, D. D., & Jeffries, F. (1995). Predictive validity and time dependency of self-efficacy, self-esteem, personal goals, and academic performance. *Educational and Psychological Measurement*, 55, 716-727.

Owens, T. (2001). *Extending self-esteem theory and research*. Cambridge: University Press.

Rosenberg, M. (1965). *Society and the adolescent self-image*. Princeton, NJ: Princeton University Press.

Thomas, R., & Chickering, A. W. (1984). Education and identity revisited. *Journal of College Student Personnel*, 25, 392-399.

Upcraft, M. L. & Schuh, J. H. (1996). *Assessment in student affairs: A guide for practitioners*. San Francisco: Jossey-Bass.

# Social Responsibility

## A. Introduction

Education is an ubiquitous phenomenon. That is, one is educated by his or her entire surroundings; everything, everywhere, at all times. And, many have pondered the purposes of education and concluded that it has both individual and collective goals.

To the individual, education is a process that results in self-development, self-awareness, and personal responsibility among other socially desirable outcomes. It is a personal experience whose ends include promotion of individual welfare and development of individual character. However, education is not exclusively an individual experience because it takes place in a social context that inextricably links the individual to the collective.

Education aims to provide disciplined, responsible citizens. Education seeks to satisfy the personal interests of the individual while preparing the individual for effective democratic social participation.

There has always been a tension between these two themes—education for individual and education for citizenship (e.g., independence vs. interdependence). However, many philosophers including John Dewey (1916) suggested that because education is a social process it represents more than the rugged individualism of the 18th century enlightenment period. Individualism must be transcended for responsible citizenship; and, education is one means of that transcendence. Social responsibility can best be described as not only an awareness of the individual-group tension, but also a call to principled action.

Social responsibility is one of the 16 student learning and development outcome domains identified by the Council for the Advancement of Standards in Higher Education (CAS). Indicators of social responsibility include participating in service or volunteer activities and understanding relevant governance systems to name a few. Social responsibility is related to and sometimes viewed as being synonymous with civic responsibility, community service, and democratic engagement.

This phenomenon is observed in different arenas—for example, politics, business, and engineering. In a political sense, social responsibility may refer to participation in governance, decision-making by voting, or actively supporting a social cause. Corporate social responsibility, on the other hand, is concerned with the relationship between business, government, and society with an emphasis on the effect of business decisions on society. And, the term has been used in engineering to underscore the importance of understanding the impact of engineering solutions in a global and societal context. Even though there are apparent contextual differences, fundamentally they focus on the individual and the collective, the unit and the universal, the human and humanity.

In many ways, social responsibility has been framed as a consequence of extracurricular community involvement. But, social responsibility is also relevant to curricular matters in the classroom. Academic programs and experiential learning opportunities should also emphasize the importance of service and civic responsibility. For example, leadership programs should not only expose students to various theories of leadership but offer experiences in the process of government and decision-making. In addition, service learning may be an effective way of increasing civic participation by incorporating community service activities with academic coursework.

It is expected that all functional area programs will emphasize learning and work to identify relevant learning outcomes. By using CAS functional area standards and guidelines, program leaders can assess student learning and development relative to social responsibility.

## B. Theoretical Contexts for Learning and Development

Student development theory is a guide for understanding what happens to students in college. It provides educators with knowledge that can be used to create interventions designed to enhance student learning and development (Evans, Forney, & Guido-Brito, 1998). Developmental theory also provides information about factors contributing to development in cognitive, affective, and behavioral domains such as social responsibility.

While there appears to be no discernable theory *explaining* social responsibility, there are a number of hypotheses *about* social responsibility. Said differently, there are a number of developmental theories that *explicate* that from which social responsibility is derived. To draw the connection, however, social responsibility must be simplified into an observable phenomenon.

Social responsibility is two words, but many things. Fundamentally, it represents an intellectual shift from a single perspective to a more complex view, a move from self to others, and from egoism to altruism. With this in mind, the work of William Perry, Lawrence Kohlberg, and Jane Loevinger are important to this discussion.

Perry (1968) examined intellectual and ethical development and set forth a theory consisting of nine positions. Essentially, his scheme is characterized by movement from a basic duality towards a more complex view of the world. Under Perry's scheme, development occurs not in the stages but during the transitions **between** stages. And, transition begins when cognitive dissonance occurs. For example, when right and wrong are not made clear or when professors do not know it all, the dualistic thinker is faced with the possibility of multiple meanings and diverse views. It is important to note that Perry's theory is not concerned with the content of one's views, but rather with the complexity involved in one's thought process.

Alongside cognitive development, Kohlberg (1969) focused on the cognitive dimensions of moral reasoning. Advancing the work of Piaget (1932, 1977), Kohlberg set forth three levels of moral reasoning: pre-conventional, conventional, and post-conventional. He suggested that each level of his theory represented a different orientation between the self and society. Essentially, the theory explains development from an individual perspective towards a more universal viewpoint.

Finally, Loevinger (1976) articulated an explanation of ego development as progressions along a continuum. Her theory, then, focuses on transition from one stage to the next. Ego development is summarized as a process of restructuring one's personality—from self-protection and opportunism to a frame of reference more integrated in community.

There is a need for additional research on social responsibility given the number of different arenas in which it is observed. Too, additional knowledge is needed to understand the relationship among social responsibility, civic engagement, and community service. Nevertheless, there is adequate information available to provide insight into development within this domain.

## C. Relevant variables

- articulates a meaning of citizenship
- understands the importance of service to others
- demonstrates an ability to make decisions
- has sense of belonging to community
- demonstrates tolerance
- challenges unfair and intolerant behavior
- understands principles of governance
- participates in community service
- has civic or historical knowledge
- cares for others
- is aware of community needs
- sees connection between self and others
- demonstrates self-awareness
- uses classroom learning in real world settings

Clearly, these variables are not exhaustive of all relevant factors related to social responsibility. Rather, this list of indicators is intended to provide a starting point for thinking about assessing student development relative to social responsibility. As it is imperative to identify dependent and independent variables early in the assessment process, this list provides the reader with several ideas of variables that might be used. The criterion (or dependent) variable essentially answers the question: What am I measuring? The predictor (or independent) variables, on the other hand, are those factors that are controlled or manipulated rather than observed. The predictor variable is often a grouping variable (for example, male versus female) and is the factor that is thought to be causal. For example, in most cases the dependent variable might be "social responsibility" while "meaning of citizenship" may be one of the independent variables.

## D. Assessment Examples

Ed G. K. Shun is the Coordinator of Service-Learning at Civic University. He is responsible for the university service-learning center and several programs including study abroad and outreach mentoring. He has a staff of two assistants and a graduate intern. They have decided to assess the effects of their service-learning project program on students' social responsibility. The following variables are of interest to them: connection between self and others (self-awareness), awareness of the needs of others (conscientiousness), and integrity. In this regard, the team considered the following approaches:

1. Quantitative: To test the hypothesis that students participating in the Service-Learning Project (SLP) would demonstrate higher levels of social responsibility, the team administered the Sentence Completion Test (SCT) (Loevinger & Wessler, 1970; Loevinger, 1996) to two groups. The control group consisted of randomly selected students who did not participate in the service-learning project. The study group consisted of those students participating regularly in the program.

   The SCT measures ego development, or operationally for this study: moral development, interpersonal relations, and conceptual complexity (Loevinger, 1998). The SCT correlates answers to open-ended responses such as "My conscience bothers me if..." and "Being with other people..." with seven stages of ego development. Data were analyzed using multiple analysis of variance (MANOVA) tests on each subscale of interest, such as "self-awareness" and "conscientiousness," to test for significant differences between the control and study groups.

   To do this, after having secured human subjects approval the coordinator and his assistants administered the SCT (Loevinger & Wessler, 1970; Loevinger, 1996) to SLP students (n=30) during a weekly meeting. In addition, the team sent electronic communication to a random sample of non-SLP students (n=30) with similar characteristics (age, year in school, etc.). After collecting the data, the team worked with the graduate assistant to input all scores in SPSS using the scoring manual (Loevinger & Wessler, 1970) for the SCT and coding all SLP students as "1" and all non-SLP students as "0" on the demographic variable "status." They ran multiple analysis of variance (MANOVA) tests on each of the variables of interest using "status" as the category of the independents. In addition they controlled for previous services experiences by asking respondents to note their previous service experience on a likert scale.

2. Qualitative: To assess the impact of this program on students' social responsibility, the team selected visual narratives (Harper, 2000) as a guiding methodology. They added several new projects to the course syllabus—in-class reflective essays, a semester log, and a photo assignment. Methodologists agree that personal documents can yield revealing information (Stage & Manning, 2003; Taylor & Bogdan, 1984). For the essay assignment, students were asked to respond to questions such as: What is the importance of community service? How does it connect you to others? What is the meaning of citizenship? In addition, students were directed to keep a written log of their service-learning experiences. Course instructors pointed out that students should record their emotions, thoughts, personal reflections, and service activities in their logs along with any new information that they learned during the semester. Finally, the culminating assignment was a photography project. Students designed display boards to reflect their entire service-learning experience using pictures, poetry, magazine clippings, and any other visual image.

Data were analyzed using document analysis that yields excerpts or quotations from the journal. To do this, the team used factual coding to identify several recurrent themes related to service-learning and social responsibility. Factual coding is a way of representing ideas that are more concrete and descriptive—for example, actions, events, settings, and processes might be selected themes. They used these themes and categorized every excerpt, quotation, or passage from the journal under a theme (Ryan & Bernard, 2000). In similar fashion, the instructors and graduate intern examined each poster board carefully and made note of any ideas or themes that related to social responsibility. Such rich, thick data are useful to understand the meaning of social responsibility from the perspective of the actual participant.

Regardless of whether quantitative, qualitative, or mixed methods are used, it is important to select an approach that will yield the kind of data needed. When implementing a quantitative approach, one should consider using institutional information previously collected and currently available. In this way, time consuming collection of new data is not required. When using a qualitative method, open-ended discussions and self-reports can be useful in yielding valuable data. There are many ways to analyze qualitative data; document analysis used in the hypothetical example is only one approach and requires a great deal of time and attention. Much qualitative data tends to go unanalyzed due to assessors being overwhelmed by the sheer volume of text involved.

It is the intention of this section to render the complex simple; realizing that a degree of accuracy is lost in the process. It must be remembered that these examples are meant to be descriptive rather than prescriptive about learning assessment. They represent only one way to assess learning and development and definitely are not the only way.

## E. Available Instruments

A word of caution…Be sure that the instruments selected yield the kind of data needed to assess the program's effectiveness. To do this, first, establish what information is essential to the analysis and then select the instrument(s) that will generate such information. The reverse should never be done. If no standardized instruments will yield the kind of data required, it is advised that an instrument be developed that will generate the kind of data needed.

*Social and Personal Responsibility Scale (SPRS)*, Conrad and Hedin, 1981.
- Assesses dimensions of responsibility along several subscales including attitudes, competence, and efficacy; 21 items
- Publisher: Dan Conrad, Center for Youth Development and Research, University of Minnesota - Twin Cities, Minneapolis, MN 5455-0213

*Career Exploration Scale (CES)*, Education Work Program, 1978.
- Focuses on actual process of exploring careers using two subscales: label action, information; 15 items.
- Publisher: Northwest Regional Laboratory (NRWL), Portland, Oregon

*Student Attitudes Questionnaire (SAQ)*, Education Work Program, 1978.
- Evaluates experience-based career education programs using self-reports about attitudes toward work; 25 items.
- Publisher: Northwest Regional Laboratory (NRWL), Portland, Oregon

*Scale of Intellectual Development (SID)*, Erwin, 1983.
- Measures intellectual development along four subscales: dualism, relativism, commitment, empathy; 119 items.
- Publisher: Developmental Analytics, P. O. Box 855, Harrisonburg, VA 22801, (703) 568-6211

*Measure of Intellectual Development (MID)*, Knefelkamp, 1974.
- Measures the first five Perry positions, 3 essays.
- Publisher: Center for the Study of Intellectual Development, The Perry Network, 1505 Farwell Ct. NW, Olympia, WA 98502, (206) 786-5094

*Measure of Epistemological Reflection (MER)*, Baxter Magolda and Porterfield, 1985.
- Measures the first five Perry positions along 6 domains of the learning process: decision-making, the role of the teacher, the role of the learner, the role of peers, evaluation, and the nature of truth.
- Publisher: Marcia B. Baxter Magolda, Department of Educational Leadership, School of Education, 350 McGuffey Hall, Miami University, Oxford, Ohio 45056, (513) 529-6825

*Moral Judgment Interview (MJI)*, Colby, Kohlberg, Speicher, Hewer, Candee, Gibbs, and Power, 1987.
- Measures moral reasoning in three hypothetical dilemmas using probe questions; structured interview format.
- Publisher: Cambridge University Press, 110 Midland Avenue, Port Chester, NY 10573-4930

*Defining Issues Test (DIT)*, Rest, 1986.
- Presents hypothetical dilemmas followed by 12 interpretations that correspond to various stages of moral reasoning; 6 items.
- Publisher: Center for the Study of Ethical Development, University of Minnesota
  206-A Burton Hall, 178 Pillsbury Drive SE, Minneapolis, MN 55455 (612) 624-0876
  For more information: http://education.umn.edu/CSED/default.html

*Sentence Completion Test (SCT)*, Loevinger, 1996.
- Measures ego development using sentence completions to elicit information about one's frame of reference; 36 items.
- Publisher: Jane Loevinger, Washington University, St. Louis, MO 63130

*Student Developmental Task and Lifestyle Assessment (SDTLA)*, Winston, Miller, and Cooper, 1999.
- Based on Chickering's Seven Vectors, the SDTLA measures college student developmental task achievement including (a) Establishing and Clarifying Purpose (52 items assessing career and lifestyle planning, cultural participation, and educational involvement); (b) Developing Autonomy (52 items measuring emotional, instrumental, and academic autonomy and interdependence); (c) Mature Interpersonal Relationships (42 items assessing tolerance, peer relationships, and salubrious life-style).
- Publisher: Student Development Associates, Inc.
- For more information: www.sdtla.appstate.edu/

Several purpose statements were adapted from those produced by the Buros Institute of Mental Measurements Test Reviews Online, www.unl.edu/buros.

## F. Related Websites

| | |
|---|---|
| National Service-Learning Clearinghouse | http://www.servicelearning.org |
| Center for Civic Education | http://www.civiced.org |
| Campus Compact | http://www.compact.org |
| AACU-Civic Engagement | http://www.aacu-edu.org/issues/civicengagement/ |
| Teaching Citizenship | http://www.ericfacility.net/databases/ERIC_Digests/ed332929.html |

## G. References

Baxter Magolda, M. B., & Porterfield, W. D. (1985). A new approach to assess intellectual development on the Perry scheme. *Journal of College Student Personnel*, 26, 343-350.

Colby, A., Kohlberg, L., Speicher, B., Hewer, A., Candee, D., Gibbs, J., & Power, C. (1987). *The measurement of moral judgment: Vol. 2. Standard Issue scoring manual.* New York: Cambridge University Press.

Conrad, D., & Hedin, D. (1981). *Social and personal responsibility scale.* St. Paul: Center for Youth Development and Research, University of Minnesota.

Dewey, J. (1916). *Democracy and education.* New York: McMillan.

Education Work Program. (1978). *Career exploration scale.* Portland: Northwest Regional Laboratory.

Education Work Program. (1978). *Student attitudes questionnaire.* Portland: Northwest Regional Laboratory.

Erwin, T. D. (1983). The Scale of Intellectual Development: Measuring Perry's scheme. *Journal of College Student Personnel*, 24, 6-12.

Evans, N. J., Forney, D. S., & Guido-Brito, F. (1998). *Student development in college: Theory, research, and practice*. San Francisco: Jossey-Bass.

Harper, D. (2000). Reimaging visual methods. In N. K. Denzin & Y. S. Lincoln (Eds.), *Handbook of qualitative research* (pp. 717-732). Thousand Oaks: Sage.

Knefelkamp, L. L. (1974). *Developmental instruction: Fostering intellectual and personal growth in college students*. Unpublished doctoral dissertation, University of Minnesota, Minneapolis.

Kohlberg, L. (1969). Stage and sequence: The cognitive developmental approach to socialization. In D. A. Goslin (Ed.), *Handbook of socialization theory and research* (pp. 347-480). Chicago: Rand McNally.

Loevinger, J., & Wessler, R. (1970). *Measuring ego development I: Construction and use of a sentence completion test* (Vol. 1). San Francisco: Jossey-Bass.

Loevinger, J. (1976). *Ego development: Conceptions and theories*. San Francisco: Jossey-Bass.

Loevinger, J. (1996). Meaning and measurement of ego development. *American Psychologist*, 21, 195-206.

Loevinger, J. (1998). History of the Sentence Completion Test (SCT) for ego development. In Loevinger, J. (Ed.) *Technical foundations for measuring ego development: The Washington University Sentence Completion Test*. Mahwah, NJ: Lawrence Erlbaum Associates.

Perry, W. G. (1968). *Forms of intellectual and ethical development in the college years: A scheme*. New York: Holt, Rinehart & Winston.

Piaget, J. (1977). *The moral judgment of the child* (M. Gabain, Trans.). Hardmondsworth, England: Penguin. (Original work published 1932)

Rest, J. R. (1986). *The Defining Issues Test (3rd ed.)*. Minneapolis: University of Minnesota, Center for the Study of Ethical Development.

Ryan, G. W., & Bernard, H. R. (2000). Data management and analysis methods. In N. K. Denzin & Y. S. Lincoln (Eds.), *Handbook of qualitative research* (pp. 769-802). Thousand Oaks, CA: Sage.

Stage, F. K., & Manning, K. (2003). *Research in the college context: Approaches and methods*. New York: Brunner-Routledge.

Taylor, S. J., & Bogdan, R. (1984). *Introduction to qualitative research methods: The search for meanings*. New York: John Wiley & Sons.

Winston, R. B., Miller, T. K., & Cooper, D. L. (1999). *Student Developmental Task and Lifestyle Assessment*. Boone, NC: Student Development Associates, Inc.

## H. Recommended Reading

Bringle, R. G., Games, R., & Malloy, E. A. (1999). *Colleges and universities as citizens*. Boston: Allyn & Bacon.

Butler, J. E. (2000). Democracy, diversity, and civic engagement. *Academe*, 86(4), 52-55.

Checkoway, B. (2000). Public service: Our new mission. *Academe*, 86(4), 24-28.

Erlich, T. (2000). *Civic responsibility and higher education*. Phoenix: Oryx Press.

Gamson, Z. F. (1997). Higher education and rebuilding civic life. *Change*, 29(1), 10-13.

Hollander, E. L., & Saltmarsh, J. (2000). The engaged university. *Academe*, 86(4), 29-32.

Maloney, W. A. (2000). The community as classroom. *Academe*, 86(4), 38-42.

Rosaen, C. L., Foster-Fishman, P., & Fear, F. (2002). The citizen-scholar: Joining voices and values in the engagement interface. *Metropolitan Universities*, 12(4), 10-28.

Zlotkowski, E. (1996). Linking service-learning and the academy. *Change*, 28, 21-27.

Upcraft, M. L, & Schuh, J. H. (1996). *Assessment in student affairs: A guide for practitioners*. San Francisco: Jossey-Bass.

Upcraft, M. L., & Schuh, J. H. (2000). *Assessment practice in student affairs: An applications manual*. San Francisco: Jossey-Bass.

# Spiritual Awareness

## A. Introduction

Spiritual awareness is one of the 16 student learning and development outcome domains identified by CAS. Indicators of spiritual awareness include the ability to develop and articulate personal belief systems and to understand the role of spirituality in personal and group values and behaviors. Spiritual awareness is often vaguely defined and viewed as being synonymous with wholeness, wellness, and religion.

One of the difficulties in defining spirituality is its intimate connection with religion, which results in the two terms often being viewed synonymously. Though they share common elements, they are significantly different (Turner, Lukoff, Barnhouse, & Lu, 1995). For example, religion often suggests adherence to the beliefs, doctrines, and practices of an organized church, denomination, or institution. Spirituality, on the other hand, refers to a quality that transcends a specific religion or faith. It relates to one's capacity to create and develop a value system. Religion may be one way in which persons express their spirituality, but it is not the same as spirituality. To most, this distinction is not clear and consequently the terms are often confused.

In many instances, student affairs professionals tend to avoid the issue of spirituality because of its close kinship to religion (Jablonski, 2001). Public higher education typically maintains a distant relationship with religion due to legalities that call for separation of church and state. However, there has been a recent surge of interest in the spiritual development of students independent of religion. As such, "student affairs professionals must understand the role that such values as faith, hope, and love play in the structure and persistence of communities, in the construction of knowledge, in the understanding of truth, and in developmental processes of students" (Love & Talbot, 1999).

Spirituality is a universal quality and relevant to both public and private institutions even though the separation of church and state is maintained. Spiritual awareness, though perhaps related to religion, can readily be framed as a process of meaning-making and achieving identity. Educators must recognize that "adult learners bring all of this with them into the learning environment" (Tisdell, 1999, p. 93). Therefore, to truly understand students, one must also understand the nature of spiritual awareness and the place of spirituality in the maturation process.

## B. Theoretical Contexts for Learning and Development

Developmental theory is useful to educators for understanding how college students grow and mature from adolescence into adulthood. Theories serve as plausible explanations of observed phenomena—including the spiritual development of students. Such theories often explain how growth and change occurs in similar fashion across various groups and characteristics (Evans, Forney, & Guido-Brito, 1998).

Few theorists have focused on spiritual development, but the work of James Fowler (1981) is well-noted in the research literature. Fowler proposed a theory that consists of a linear progression of stepwise stages, referred to as *stages of faith*. The six stages of faith include (a) intuitive/projective faith, (b) mythic/literal faith, (c) synthetic/conventional faith, (d) individuative/projective faith, (e) conjunctive faith, and (f) universalizing faith.

The latter three stages are most relevant for student affairs professionals working with college-age students and adult learners. In stage four, students step out of the interpersonal community to which they belong and reflect upon self and others, "my group," and other groups. Stage five is marked by a critical examination of the unconscious that powerfully shapes lives. Stage six, which few people actually achieve, is characterized by a shift from "self as center" to a more universal reality.

Fowler (1981) spoke of faith as a process of meaning-making, which implies making sense out of the activities of life, seeking patterns, order, coherence, and relation between and among the disparate elements of human living. Faith can refer to either religious or non-religious faith and, according to Fowler, is a characteristic of all human beings. In this way, faith is as universal and varied as language and culture.

Fowler's theory is particularly useful to educators interested in understanding or measuring the spiritual awareness of students by looking specifically at the way they construct their faith. Less emphasis is placed upon the *content* of one's faith, but rather the way in which one structures his or her faith is emphasized (Parrott & Steele, 1995). In this sense, spiritual development is both cognitive and psychosocial as it refers to the way in which students "come to know life's meaning."

Psychosocially, spiritual development is related to issues of identity and change throughout the human life span. Erikson (1975) said that humans continue to develop throughout life via eight stages of development. Each developmental stage consists of life challenges or crises that must be resolved. Crisis, in this sense, is not so much a catastrophic event as it is a necessary and normal tension or struggle that, when resolved in a timely fashion, results in developmental transition and growth. In this way, successful resolution of spiritual matters results in increasingly greater levels of spiritual awareness.

Several researchers have expanded upon Fowler's work (Helminiak, 1987; Parks, 2000) and many others have used his work as a framework for their research on spiritual development (Love, 2002; Love & Talbot, 1999; Stewart, 2002). It is clear that additional knowledge is needed about how spiritual development occurs as well as whether spiritual awareness and spirituality are synonymous. Nevertheless, there is adequate information available to guide the measurement of development within this domain.

## C. Relevant Variables

- has a personal view of the meaning of life
- recognizes a connection of living entities
- recognizes the role of religion
- has resilience
- has purpose of life
- seeks a sense of meaning
- attends events that enhance spirituality
- demonstrates compassion
- is self-aware
- prays, meditates or reflects in other ways

Clearly, these variables are not exhaustive of all relevant variables related to spiritual awareness. Rather, this list of indicators is intended to provide a starting point for thinking about assessing the spiritual dimensions of learning. As it is imperative to identify dependent and independent variables early in the assessment process, this list provides the reader with several ideas of variables that might be used. The criterion (or dependent) variable essentially answers the question: What am I measuring? The predictor (or independent) variables, on the other hand, are those factors that are controlled or manipulated rather than observed. The predictor variable is often a grouping variable (for example, male versus female) and is the factor that is thought to be causal. For example, in most cases the dependent variable might be "spiritual awareness" while "purpose and meaning of life" may be one of the independent variables. Spirituality is fundamentally about meaning-making and this leads one on a personal search for meaning in life.

## D. Assessment Examples

Ewell B. Good is the acting Director of Student Activities as Westeastern University. In this position, he oversees several programs including a leadership development program called "Leaders in the Making (LIM)." He and a team of staff members decided to assess this program's affect on students' spiritual awareness. First, they operationalized spiritual awareness as a process of meaning-making. They chose belief in a higher power, purpose and meaning of life, resilience, and self-awareness as the independent variables. The team considered the following approaches:

1. Quantitative: To test the hypothesis that students participating in LIM would demonstrate higher levels of spiritual awareness, after securing human subjects approval the team administered the Spirituality Assessment Scale (Howden, 1992) to two groups. The control group consisted of randomly selected students who did not participate in the leadership program. The study group consisted of those students participating regularly in the leadership program. Data were analyzed using one-way ANOVA on each variable of interest, such as "belief in a higher power," to test for significant differences between the control and experimental groups. Alternatively, the relationship could be studied using regression analyses.

2. Qualitative: To explore how students grow in spiritual awareness, the team decided to ask each participant to respond to questions as part of a weekly journal assignment: These questions included: What things do you believe in that give meaning to your life? What role might your religion/spirituality play in resolving your problems? In what ways do you experience life as a part of a greater whole, in what ways do you not?

    Using a grounded theory methodology, data were analyzed using document analysis that yields excerpts or quotations from the journal (document). To do this, the team used a form of coding called axial coding. Axial coding builds connections between categories and subcategories. Specifically, they identified recurrent categories in the documents related to spiritual awareness and looked for ways to combine and collapse categories. This led to the development of categories and subcategories. In the final analysis, responses were used to create a theory of spiritual development of these participants (Glaser & Strauss, 1967).

Regardless of whether quantitative, qualitative, or mixed methods are used, it is important to select an approach that will yield the kind of data needed. If using a quantitative approach, consider using institutional information already available. In this way, new data may not need to be collected. If using a qualitative method, open-ended discussions and self-reports can be useful in yielding valuable data. There are many ways to analyze qualitative data; document analysis is only one example and requires a great deal of time and attention. Much qualitative data goes without being analyzed due to researchers being overwhelmed by the sheer volume of text involved. Finally, in this section, it is our intention to render the complex simple, realizing that we give up a degree of accuracy in the attempt.

## E. Available instruments

A word of caution...Be sure that these instruments yield the kind of data that you need to assess your program's effectiveness. To do this, first, determine what you want to know and then go about finding an instrument that will provide you with such information. Do not do the reverse. If none of these instruments yield the kind of data that you are interested in, you are advised to develop your own instrument to meet your needs.

*Inventory of Religious Activities and Interests (IRAI)* by Webb and Hunt, 1968.
- Measures interest in activities performed by persons employed in a variety of church-related occupations.
- Publisher: Ministry Inventories, ATTN: Richard A. Hunt, Ph.D., Fuller Graduate School of Psychology, 180 N. Oakland Avenue, Pasadena, CA 91101; Educational Testing Service (ETS), Princeton, NJ.
- For more information: http://www.buros.unl.edu/buros

*Spiritual Well-Being Scale* by Ellison, 1983.
- Measures spiritual well-being as a two-dimensional construct: religious well-being and existential well-being. Religious well-being refers to the concept of God; existential well-being relates to the purpose of life independent of religion; 20 items.
- Publisher: Life Advance, Inc., 81 Front Street, Nyack, NY 10960; Telephone: 914-358-2539; Email: Ellison@alliancesem.edu
- For more information: http://www.adventist.org.ru/psyh/rs_psp02.htm

*Wellness Inventory* by National Wellness Institute, Inc., 1992.
- Designed to promote awareness of individual and group wellness that measures wellness along six dimensions: physical, social, occupational, spiritual, emotional, and intellectual; 100 items.
- Publisher: National Wellness Institute, Inc., 1300 College Court, PO Box 827, Stevens Point, WI 54481-2962
- For more information: http://www.testwell.org

*Values Preference Indicator (VPI)* by Robinson, 1990.
- Provides respondents with the tools to examine their values and priorities for the purpose of self-learning, group discussion, team development and gaining insight into corporate culture.
- Publisher: Consulting Resource Group International, Inc., #386-200 West Third Street, Sumas, WA 98295-8000
- For more information: www.crgleader.com/product/123/Online_Values_Preference_Indicator.html

Several purpose statements were adapted from those produced by the Buros Institute of Mental Measurements Test Reviews Online, www.unl.edu/buros.

## F. Related Websites

| | |
|---|---|
| ASERVIC | www.aservic.org |
| Ananda Online | http://www.ananda.org |
| Divine Way of Spiritual Heart | http://www.swami-center.org |
| Spiritual Development | http://www.csp.org/development/development.html |
| Spiritual Development and Healing | http://www.holisticmed.com/www/spirit.html |
| World Congress of Faiths | http://www.worldfaiths.org |

# G. References

Ellison, C. W. (1983). Spiritual well-being: Conceptualization and measurement. *Journal of Psychology and Theology*, 14, 330-340.

Evans, N. J., Forney, D. S., & Guido-Brito, F. (1998). *Student development in college: Theory, research, and practice.* San Francisco: Jossey-Bass.

Erikson, E. H. (1975). *Life history and the historical moment.* New York: Norton.

Fowler, J. (1981). *Stages of faith: The psychology of human development and the quest for meaning.* New York: Harper & Row.

Glaser, B. G. & Strauss, A.L. (1967/1999). *Discovery of grounded theory: Strategies for qualitative research.* Chicago: Aldine.

Helminiak, D. A. (1987). *Spiritual development: An interdisciplinary study.* Chicago: Loyola University Press.

Howden, J. W. (1992). *Development and psychometric characteristics of the spirituality assessment scale.* Unpublished doctoral dissertation. Texas Women's University.

Jablonski, M. A. (2001). The implications of student spirituality for student affairs practice. *New Directions for Student Services*, 95, 1-5.

Love, P. G. (2002). Comparing spiritual development and cognitive development. *Journal of College Student Development*, 43(3), 357-373.

Love, P., & Talbot, D. (1999). Defining spiritual development: A missing consideration for student affairs. *NASPA Journal*, 37, 361-375.

Parks, S. (2000). *Big questions, worthy dreams: Mentoring young adults in their search for meaning, purpose, and faith.* San Francisco: Jossey-Bass.

Parrott, L., & Steele, L. (1995). Integrating psychology and theology at undergraduate colleges: A developmental perspective. *Journal of Psychology and Theology*, 23(4), 261-265.

Robinson, E. T. (1990). *Values preference indicator.* Sumas, WA: Consulting Resource Group.

Stewart, D. L. (2002). The role of faith in the development of an integrated identity: A qualitative study of Black students at a White college. *Journal of College Student Development*, 43(4), 579-595.

Tisdell, E. J. (1999). The spiritual dimension of adult development. In M. C. Clark and R. S. Caffarella (Eds.), An update on adult development theory: New ways of thinking about the life course (pp. 87-96). *New Directions of Adult Development*, Number 84. San Francisco: Jossey-Bass.

Turner, R. P., Lukoff, D., Barnhouse, R. T., & Lu, F. G. (1995). Religious or spiritual problem. *Journal of Nervous and Mental Disease*, 183(7), 435-444.

Webb, S., & Hunt, R. A. (1968). *Inventory of Religious Activities and Interests.* Princeton, NJ: Educational Testing Service.

## H. Recommended reading

Banta, T., Lund, J. P., Black, K. E., & Oblander, F. W. (1996). *Assessment in practice: Putting principles to work on college campuses.* San Francisco: Jossey-Bass.

Bryant, A. N., Choi, J. Y., & Yasuno, M. (2003). Understanding the religious and spiritual dimensions of students' lives in the first year of college. *Journal of College Student Development,* 44(6), 723-745.

Corbett, J. M. (1990). *Religion in America.* Englewood Cliffs, NJ: Prentice-Hall.

Elkins, D. N., Hedstrom, L. J., Hughes, L. L., Leaf, J. A., & Saunders, C. (1988). Toward a humanistic-phenomenological spirituality. *Journal of Humanistic Psychology,* 28, 5-18.

Fowler, J. (1981). *Stages of faith: The psychology of human development and the quest for meaning.* New York: Harper & Row.

Hill, P. C., & Hood, R. W. (1999). *Measures of religiosity.* Birmingham, AL: Religious Education Press.

Hood, R. W., Spilka, B., Hunsberger, B., & Gorsuch, R. (1996). *The psychology of religion: An empirical approach.* New York: Guilford Press.

Kelly, E. W. (1995). *Spirituality and religion in counseling and psychotherapy: Diversity in theory and practice.* Alexandria, VA: American Counseling Association.

Newman, L. L. & Smith, C. (Eds.). (Spring 2004). Special Issue: Faith, spirituality, & religion on campus. *College Student Affairs Journal,* 23(2), 97-218.

Rodgers, J. L, & Dantley, M. E. (2001). Invoking the spiritual in campus life and leadership. *Journal of College Student Development,* 42(6), 589-603.

Upcraft, M. L, & Schuh, J. H. (1996). *Assessment in student affairs: A guide for practitioners.* San Francisco: Jossey-Bass.

Upcraft, M. L., & Schuh, J. H. (2000). *Assessment practice in student affairs: An applications manual.* San Francisco: Jossey-Bass.

# Clarified Values

## A. Introduction

The word "value" is from the Latin word "valere" meaning to be worthy or strong. Values are defined as desirable qualities and that which is prized, esteemed, or highly regarded as good. For example, good is a value while evil is the opposite of a value often called a disvalue (Angeles, 1992). Values are important when determining or judging the worth of experiences. Dewey (1916) suggested that every adult in the course of his or her education acquires certain measures for deciding the worth of experiences. Education, then, encourages a person to appreciate values such as honesty, perseverance, and loyalty over disvalues like lying and hatred.

There are both intrinsic and extrinsic values. Intrinsic values have internal and personal significance. Faith is an intrinsic value as it may be important and apparent to the individual only. Extrinsic values have external significance and may be apparent to others. For example, compassion may be considered as an extrinsic value. Intrinsic or extrinsic, values are important and shape attitudes, behaviors, and decisions. Kohlberg (1969) identified several universal values including family, community, property, and the sanctity of life.

Pascarella and Terenzini (2005) stated in their seminal work, *How College Affects Students*, "Since the founding of Harvard College in 1636, American higher education has been deeply involved in shaping student attitudes, values, and beliefs" (p. 271). It is, in fact, the role of education to transmit values and shape student attitudes and beliefs.

High school students, their parents, and those who work in higher education may have different feelings about college and reasons for going, but most agree that going to college is important and serves a number of personal and societal goals. Educators should remember that education has both public and private benefits—that is, it adds to the value of the individual and the collective. In this domain, education helps individuals clarify their own values and therefore influences the nature of society's values at the same time.

## B. Theoretical Contexts for Learning and Development

Axiology is the study of or theory of values. The Greek translation of axiology suggests that it is the study of "worth" or worthiness. Axiology is the analysis of values to determine their meaning, characteristics, origins, types, criteria, and epistemological status (Angeles, 1992).

There are three basic perspectives on values: (a) objectivity theory, (b) relativity of values, and (c) subjectivity theory. Objectivity theory suggests that values exist in the real world and can be understood as real entities and qualities. In the same way, values can be supported by rational argumentation as being the best under various circumstances. The relative theory of values suggests that values are relative to social and personal preferences. These preferences include attitudes, tastes, and feelings to name a few. In this frame, values are conditioned by one's environment and/or culture. Therefore, values differ from culture to culture and orthodox value judgments (e.g., right and wrong) cannot be made.

Similar to relativity of values, subjectivity theory purports that values are subjective and do not exist in an objective world. From that perspective, there are no universal, absolute, and objective values applicable to all. Values are contextual and conditioned by time and space.

Hyman and Wright (1979) provided seminal evidence on the enduring effects of education on values. They argued that exploring the effects of education on values moves the discussion away from education's influence on knowledge and towards its effects on both knowledge and character. Given the definition of a value, they tried to include values whose moral worth is largely agreed upon. For example, peace, harmony, freedom, liberty, equality, truth, and love were included in the analyses. Results suggested that education and experiences during college may have an enduring effect on post-college life.

## C. Relevant Variables

- articulates personal values
- makes decisions that reflect personal values
- identifies personal, work, and lifestyle values
- distinguishes values from interests
- acts in congruence with personal values
- demonstrates willingness to scrutinize personal beliefs and values
- explains how values influence decision-making
- understands the role of society in shaping values

This list of variables is by no means an exhaustive list of all of the relevant variables associated with clarified values. Rather, it is intended to provide a point of departure for thinking about assessing the dimensions of learning related to clarified values.

As it is imperative to identify variables early in the assessment process, this list provides the reader with several variables that might be used. As a general rule, the criterion (or dependent) variable essentially answers the question: What am I measuring? The predictor (or independent) variables, on the other hand, are those factors that are controlled or manipulated rather than observed. The predictor variable is often a grouping variable (for example, gender or year in college) and is the factor that is thought to be causal. For example, in most cases the dependent variable is the learning outcome while "identifies personal values" may be one of the independent variables.

## D. Assessment Examples

Dr. Bea Goode is head of the Women's Center at Big Rock College. During a recent staff meeting, Dr. Goode and her staff members discussed an article they had read. The article suggested that women, between the ages of 18 and 28, tend to place masculine values above their own and feel insecure around men and other women. For Women's Month, Dr. Goode and her staff consistently sponsor a number of panel discussions, keynote speakers, book sessions, and a two-day conference to address women's issues including women's values and self-esteem. To obtain data on the influence of these programs on women's values, the team considered the following two approaches:

1. Quantitative: To measure the effects of Women's Month programs on women's values, the team administered the *Hall-Tonna Inventory of Values* to all women who attended the two-day conference. First, participants were asked to provide demographic information and to indicate which programs they attended during

Women's Month. Second, participants were asked to identify present value priorities as measured by the inventory. Third, respondents were asked to indicate whether attending Women's Month events influenced their value priorities. In this section, participants noted if their value priorities had changed and, if so, identified the program(s) that effected such changes.

2. Qualitative: To collect qualitative data, the team adopted an ethnographical design (Ellis & Bochner, 2000) as they considered the conference a quasi "culture." Fifteen women who attended the Women's Month conference were selected through a process of snowball sampling. Each assessment participant was asked to respond to the following questions in an essay: "Have your values (and value priorities) changed as a result of Women's Month events? If so, how? If not, why not?" Participants also involved in focus group discussions. Groups responses were transcribed. After collecting responses, the team (a) assigned each essay to two reviewers as a way of triangulating investigators (Denzin, 1978); (b) read each transcript thoroughly several times making note of words identifying learning, development, and values; (c) created categories of these terms; (d) used the categories to analyze the influence of culture of Women's Month activities on values, and (e) used member checking as a way of ensuring trustworthiness (Lincoln & Guba, 2000).

## E. Available Instruments

A word of caution—be certain that these instruments yield the type of data that you need to measure learning and development in this domain. To do this, first determine what you want to know and then search for the instrument that will provide you with such information. Do not do the reverse. If none of these instruments yield the kind of data that you are interested in, you are advised to develop your own instrument to meet your specific needs.

*College Outcome Measures Program (COMP)* by Forrest & Steele, n.d.
- Standardized measure designed to assess the general education outcomes of college.
- Publisher: ACT, Inc., 2201 N. Dodge Street, P.O. Box 168, Iowa City, IA 52243.
- For more information: www.unl.edu/buros; www.act.org

*Assessor Employment Values Inventory* by Selby Millsmith Ltd, n.d.
- Measure of personal values relative to work and the work environment.
- Publisher: Penna Assessment c/o Penna Change Consulting, The Manor House, Park Road, Stoke Page, Bucks, SL2 4PG, United Kingdom.
- For more information: www.unl.edu; www.e-penna.com/change

*Career Anchors: Discovering your real values, Revised Edition* by Schein, n.d.
- Designed to identify career anchors and values to use in the decision process.
- Publisher: Jossey-Bass, A Wiley Company, 989 Market Street, San Franscisco, CA 94103.
- For more information: www.unl.edu/buros

*Hall-Tonna Inventory of Values* by Brian Hall, Benjamin Tonna, Oren Harari, Barbara Ledig, and Murray Tondow, n.d.
- Inventory used to identify present value priorities and what is needed for future growth in this area.
- Publisher: Behaviordyne, Inc., publisher address is unavailable.
- For more information: www.unl.edu/buros

*Motives, Values, Preferences Inventory* by Joyce Hogan and Robert Hogan, n.d.
- Designed to evaluate the congruence between an individual and an organization in terms of motives and values.
- Publisher: Hogan Assessment Systems, Inc., P.O. Box 521176, Tulsa, OK 74152.
- For more information: www.unl.edu/buros

*Personal Values Questionnaire* by Joni Funk and Richard Mansfield, n.d.
- Measures individuals values in three areas: achievement, affiliation, and power.
- Publisher: Hay Group, Hay Resources Direct, 116 Huntington Avenue, Boston, MA, 02116.
- For more information: www.unl.edu/buros; www.hayresourcesdirect.haygroup.com

Several purpose statements were adapted from those produced by the Buros Institute of Mental Measurements Test Reviews Online, www.unl.edu/buros.

## F. Related Websites

| | |
|---|---|
| Values Activity Guide | www.help-yourself.com/values |
| David Vrensk Values Exercise | www.cling.gu.se/~cl2david/misc/robin.html |
| Paper: Values Clarification | www.sntp.net/education/values_clar.htm |
| Lifestride: Values Clarification | www.lifestrides.com/valuesclarification.htm |
| Virtue, Ethics, & Core Values | www.usafa.af.mil/jscope/JSCOPE99/Tiel99.html |
| Leader Values | www.leader-values.com |
| Princeton University Center for Human Values | www.princeton.edu/~uchv |
| Mytho Self Training Materials | www.mythoself.com |
| Values: McGregor's Values Theory | www.teleometrics.com/infor/resources_xy.html |
| Journal of College and Character | http://www.collegevalues.org/journal.cfm |

## G. References

Angeles, P. A. (1992). *The Harper Collins Dictionary of Philosophy (2nd ed.)*. New York: Harper Collins Publishers.

Denzin, N. K. (1978). *The research act: A theoretical introduction to sociological methods (2nd ed.)*. New York: McGraw-Hill.

Dewey, J. (1916). *Democracy and education*. New York: McMillan.

Ellis, C., & Bochner, A. P. (2000). Autoethnography, personal narrative, reflexivity: Researcher as subject. In N. K. Denzin & Y. S. Lincoln (Eds.), *Handbook of qualitative research* (pp. 733-768). Thousand Oaks, CA: Sage.

Hyman, H. H., & Wright, C. R. (1979). *Education's lasting influence on values*. Chicago: The University of Chicago Press.

Kohlberg, L. (1969). Stage and sequence: The cognitive development approach to socialization. In D. A. Goslin (Ed.), *Handbook of socialization theory and research* (pp. 347-480). Chicago: Rand McNally.

Lincoln, Y. S., & Guba, E. G. (1985). *Naturalistic inquiry*. Beverly Hills, CA: Sage.

Pascarella, E. T., & Terenzini, P. T. (2005). *How college affects students, Volume 2*. San Francisco: Jossey-Bass.

## H. Recommended Reading

Baer, R. A. (1982). Teaching values in schools. *American Education*, 18(9), 11-17.

Hodge, R. L. (1989). *A myriad of values: A brief history*.

Kilpatrick, W. (1992). *Why Johnny can't tell right from wrong*. New York: Simon & Schuster.

Kirschenbaum, H. (1992). A comprehensive model for values education and moral education. *Phi Delta Kappan*, 73(10), 771-776.

Lickona, T. (1993). The return of character education. *Educational Leadership*, 51(3), 6-11.

Ryan, K. (1986). The new moral education. *Phi Delta Kappan*, 68(4), 19-24.

# Epilogue

The Frameworks for Assessing Learning and Development Outcomes (FALDOs) presented in the previous 16 chapters represent an effort by the Council for the Advancement of Standards in Higher Education (CAS) to assist practitioners in carrying out assessment, an increasingly necessary educational activity. The main purpose of this closing chapter is to highlight follow through activities that are essential to the completion of meaningful assessment efforts. Assessment is intended to generate valuable data or information. This chapter focuses on uses of such data.

All Frameworks are presented in a similar format and structure. An introduction section presents general information about a specified learning domain and outlines how the outcome can be enhanced through education. This is followed by a discussion of the theoretical underpinnings associated with each domain. In some instances, human developmental theory is used as the basis for explaining how learning and growth occur in a particular domain. In other instances, the discussion rests upon theories and models from other academic disciplines such as mass communication and social learning.

Every attempt has been made to present readers with useful and measurable variables that can be incorporated readily into an assessment project. These variables serve as indicators of growth and development; they are often closely related to scales and subscales on standardized measurement instruments. Section D of each Framework outlines two detailed assessment examples—one using quantitative techniques, the other using qualitative methods of inquiry.

To bring the list of variables and the assessment examples together, Section E identified a number of measurement instruments relevant to the domain under consideration for positivistic studies. Each instrument, often a self-report survey tool, is described as to its purpose, scales and subscales (if relevant), number of items, and authors. In addition, details about the publisher including name, location, and contact information are provided.

The final two sections consisted of references and recommended readings and are provided as resources to those who desire additional information about a particular learning domain. The references referred to works cited in the Framework while the recommended readings were especially selected as relevant resources for further study.

## The Future of Assessment

Recent decades have been marked by increased accountability demands from governmental agencies, accrediting bodies, and the public at large for concrete evidence indicating what students learn and can do upon earning a college degree. The purposes of a college education have been challenged by various constituent groups including politicians, prospective employers, higher education observers, parents, and even students. And, in all likelihood, members of the higher education community believe in the need for such accountability in their institutions. Successful education makes meaning of the learning that takes place inside and outside the classroom.

Learning how to learn, think critically, make intelligent decisions, and function effectively in the larger community are all very important considerations for educators in higher education. In effect, learning outcomes assessment is an excellent vehicle for providing the information needed to ascertain what students are gaining from the college experience and, perhaps of greatest importance, to measure the impact of informal education on all students, even those whose recalcitrance to formal learning may well short-circuit their education before formal fruition.

Although some educators would rather work with academically interested and inquisitive students than with recalcitrant or unenthusiastic ones, all students admitted to an institution deserve reasonably equal treatment as well as opportunity. Many students are virtually lost when initially exposed to the higher education milieu although most ultimately mature to a point where they are able to both cope and succeed academically. Others accommodate to the higher education process quickly and flourish in the educational "garden" and sometimes even stimulate growth in the faculty and staff members with whom they interact. Most academics thrive on such students and bask in the opportunity to encourage and guide such enthusiastic learners. However, there are other students who, in order to succeed academically, need special attention, encouragement, and support. Such students may well require non-traditional, alternative approaches by those who seek to educate and otherwise enhance their learning and development. Somehow the higher education community must be increasingly flexible and creative in serving all students, traditional and non-traditional and especially those who face the tasks of determining who they are, where they are going, and how they plan to arrive at a chosen destination.

Too many college students withdraw from school prematurely while some graduate but without the requisite skills and competencies required for gainful employment and successful living. An unfortunate few even obtain degrees because of external pressures with academic learning being largely irrelevant and secondary to extrinsic rewards. Students such as these represent a unique challenge to educators because they may require developmental educators to reach out to these students to take fuller advantage of the opportunities provided. And, even if these students fail to adjust to the higher education experience in a traditional sense, personal learning and development can be enhanced via a healthy educational engendering community in such a way as to provide them with opportunities to learn and develop in a non-traditional context.

In effect, all students are unique and have special needs that may require extraordinary approaches to meet. The outcomes assessment process, therefore, has as much, if not more, utility for determining college impact as it does for more traditional, academically inclined students.

As the hue and cry for accountability increases, so too does the need for student outcomes assessment which is an intensive, strategic process of planning, gathering, analyzing, and reporting information to document *what* students learn and *how* they develop as a direct result of the college experience. Outcomes are the measurable knowledge and awareness domains, skills, and abilities that a college education affords. These learnings range from marketable skills (e.g., writing effectively, speaking clearly) to more affective gains such as appreciating diversity, interacting comfortably with others, and becoming spiritually aware.

The demands for accountability and the press for student outcomes assessment will increasingly influence higher education. Today, institutions of higher learning operate in an evidence-based assessment-driven context and therefore the need to demonstrate the effects of college on students will characterize the decades ahead. As the economy ebbs and flows, the need to justify federal, state, and private investments in education will increase. Additional evidence will be needed to justify the development and implementation of additional student services and support programs to meet the needs of traditionally underrepresented groups and other "new students." Given this trend, educators clearly need to become comfortable with assessment data—how to collect, interpret, and use such data.

## Interpretations and Uses of Assessment Data

Put simply, assessment yields results and such results come in various forms. Some may be generated as survey data and others as observational data. All can be useful and all can be interpreted.

Given the multiple forms of assessment data, one can use a mixture of strategies referred to as mixed methods studies. Interpretation must be creative and fresh. For example, results from the *Sentence Completion Test* (Loevinger & Wessler, 1970) provide information about ego development. However, the data may be paired with results from other ego measurement scales to provide a richer understanding of this developmental phenomenon and for validity purposes.

In fact, results from the *Sentence Completion Test* might be coupled with observational data of an ethnographic study to provide a rich, thick description of ego development among a given sample. Those who truly desire to implement "in depth" student learning and development assessments are strongly encouraged to consider multiple interpretations of assessment data. Likewise, the involvement of multiple constituents, such as faculty members, in the interpretation of assessment results is strongly advocated. Faculty members, especially those schooled in the social sciences and human research strategies can bring valuable expertise to assessment projects and may prove helpful when interpreting findings. Just as the use of multiple measurement tools strengthens data collection, a broadened group of eyes and diagnostic minds can enhance both the content and quality of the interpretational process.

Interpreting assessment data can be a complex task. Interpretation of such data requires more than merely analyzing and describing the information using statistical means. It also involves explaining the meaning of data in practical terms and highlighting recommendations based on findings.

Assessment data has great utility for continuous improvement and the reform/renewal of the educational process. What is done should respond to and reflect what is known. The more that is known about the effects of college on students, the more educators are able to create enhanced living and working environments that promote student learning and development effectively. Richer and more stimulating environments can be intentionally established when available data are used to guide and frame their creation.

As a number of learning and developmental theorists (Astin, 1977, 1984; Baxter Magolda, 2001, 2003; Belenky, Clinchy, Goldberger & Tarule, 1986; Dewey, 1916; Heath, 1968; Lewin, 1936; Perry, 1968; Piaget, 1952; Sanford, 1967; Strange & Banning, 2001) have postulated, when students are provided stimulation they will invariably respond. When they receive support within that context of stimulation and response, change occurs. The intelligent interpretation of relevant outcomes data can determine changes in understanding, thinking, leading, interacting, and healthy behavior, among other domains. Some of those changes are attitudinal and affective in nature as well as intellectual and competence based.

Reporting is another central consideration of any assessment initiative. Erwin (1991) described the process as "who says what and how to whom" (p. 133). Reporting then consists of four factors: the source, the method of presentation, the report, and the audience.

Generally, either faculty members, student affairs professionals, administrators and institutional researchers, serve as the source of assessment reports. This is often determined by one's expertise, contextual knowledge, objectivity, and ability to collaborate (Brown, 1978; Erwin, 1991). Because, the source of assessment information can significantly affect the way in which results are used, the source must be deemed credible.

The method of presentation can also influence the degree to which results and recommendations are implemented. Passon (1987) identified five reporting methods: progress reports, final reports, technical reports, summary reports, and media presentations. The type of report should meet the goals of the assessment.

Erwin (1991) set forth a framework for what is to be included in assessment reports. Using his framework as a base, CAS recommends the following list as a topics to include: (a) objectives or what was assessed, (b) methods or how the objectives were assessed, (c) results and conclusions including recommendations, (d) uses of data, and (e) implications for future research, policy, and practice.

Because, all programs have limitations and problems, reports should provide balanced judgments about a program's effectiveness and realistic appraisals of the impact of college on students. College environments can have a limited to no effect on a particular outcome of interest. "No effect" results should be reported.

Wergin (1989) and others pointed out that there are no real "negative" findings in assessment work. Given the fact that assessment is best used for program improvement and measuring student learning, all findings can have a positive effect on such purposes. For example, consider a student affairs professional who conducts a study to determine if the objectives of his or her first -year seminar course are being met. If he or she finds that few students demonstrate such learning at the end of the course, the instructor still learns much. Findings should identify positive effects as well as highlight areas of improvement.

To this end, assessment findings must be reported in such a way that their utility is maximized. This requires trust, open communication, continuous feedback loops, involvement of various constituents including those internal and external to the institution or program, and sensitivity to the particular needs of the assessment audience (e.g., policymakers, accreditation associations, parents, etc.) (Erwin, 1991). Assessment reports are nothing more than ornaments on a service provider's desk if they stop short of implementation. Reports must be written and presented in such a way as to increase the chances of its use. Therefore, a bit of creativity, various reporting strategies, and graphics may be needed. For example, stories can have powerful effects on policymaker and parents. In addition to producing a technical summary report of an assessment study, one may consider presenting a collection of students' stories. Reports can be used to maximize the various ways in which assessment results can be used.

Assessment results have special utility for both program and institution-wide accreditation purposes. In fact, virtually all accrediting bodies have established standards and performance indicators as benchmarks. FALDOs provide guidance about conducting assessments to supply accrediting bodies and others with relevant evidence. CAS FALDO outcomes assessment data has great utility for accrediting agency's requirements as well as for enhancing the substance and quality of institutional programs and services. Creating regular periodic reports using the CAS standards and FALDOs will lessen considerably the stress that often accompanies accreditation self-studies. If a program or an institution has collected assessment data for a period of several years, there will be minimal need for creating and implementing new assessment projects to meet accreditation reaffirmation requirements. Initiating annual outcomes assessment projects and using the results to guide innovative practices are considered by institutional leaders as "cutting edge" administrative practice.

Finally, data generated via the FALDOs is especially important for providing learning and developmental feedback to students. Students tend to become increasingly involved in programs and activities in which they have opportunities to test their abilities to take on leadership roles, serve student government, advise peers, and become involved in other student life programs. Involvement in such campus activities provides students with many opportunities for informal learning and development. Providing students with concrete assessment data that can be used in student portfolios or developmental transcripts (Brown & DeCoster, 1982) can be an added benefit to students who become so involved.

## Implications and Conclusions

This set of 16 CAS Frameworks was designed to provide a tool to educators, who are concerned with assessing student learning and development across a broad range of outcomes. As previously mentioned, this volume was not written to be read sequentially, cover-to-cover. Instead, most readers will wish to read the introductory chapters and the epilogue first, then pick and choose the Frameworks that relate most closely to the learning and development domains in which they are especially interested in pursuing in their outcomes assessment activity.

Nevertheless, it is strongly suggested that professionals review all 16 FALDOs carefully to ascertain which ones have greatest relevance to the functional area under consideration. Although it is unrealistic to expect all functional areas to assess student outcomes in each and every learning and development domain, there is ample reason to believe that multiple domains are influenced by virtually all functional area programs and services. For instance, career service programs will influence students' development in domains other than the Career Development domain including realistic self appraisal and satisfying productive lifestyles. Program leaders are strongly encouraged to consider how their services and projects impact student learning and development in several domains.

This volume has implications for those who work in programs and services whose purposes are closely related to the institution's educational mission. Increasingly, educators are expected to document their contributions to the institution's academic mission and to provide evidence that their work truly impacts student learning and development. Each Framework functions as a guide to assist practitioners in conducting quality assessment projects that yield meaningful outcomes evidence. For example, using the *Social Responsibility* FALDO, Greek affairs administrators may consider investigating the effects of Greek involvement on member's understanding of community, citizenship, or awareness of and regard for others. Often students who are members of Greek organizations participate in community service projects. These activities may affect students' sense of social responsibility.

Practitioners who work in campus ministries might also find material in this volume particularly useful. For example, spiritual awareness is an area of study that has received increased attention from educators in recent years. Those who work in campus ministries may use the *Spiritual Awareness* FALDO as a guide for assessing effects of their work on students' learning and development. In addition, spiritual awareness need not be the only campus ministry assessment concern. For example, campus ministries often sponsor student fellowships and community activities. It may be relevant to assess the effects of such involvement on students' interpersonal skills, self esteem, and communication abilities.

The FALDOs are designed to complement previous volumes published by CAS including *The Book of Professional Standards for Higher Education* and the *Self-Assessment Guides (SAGs)*. The FALDOs represent an initiative that will require review and updating continuously. Expanded iterations of some FALDOs are being considered for future promulgation.

This book of FALDOs has utility to serve as a useful complement to a textbook on assessment and evaluation. Graduate preparation program faculty members may wish to consider using this text in conjunction with commonly used research methods and evaluation handbooks when teaching courses on assessment or program evaluation. The practical assessment examples, lists of variables, and available instruments will, in many instances, provide additional information not addressed in other more traditional textbooks and user manuals.

Several limitations should be noted. Each of the 16 CAS FALDOs presented herein is organized around the learning domains identified by CAS. Other organizations have suggested alternative definitions of learning domains. For example, see *Learning Reconsidered* (ACPA and NASPA, 2004), where there is remarkable resemblance and overlap between the CAS identified domains. The 16 CAS FALDOs do not speak to all possible domains or interpretations.

In addition, this work was written from the perspective of student affairs professionals and other student support service educators (e.g., academic advisors, conference and events providers, learning assistance educators, educational opportunity staff members, and women student program educators). The examples may be of less use to those working in non-campus settings or non-student support areas, though the introduction and theoretical discussions are designed to have utility for all educators.

Despite such limitations, the FALDOs are provided as outcomes assessment tools with the intent of being a valuable resource to those concerned with measuring student learning and development in college contexts. It is a work-in-progress that seeks to address most central considerations of learning outcomes assessment.

# References

ACPA and NASPA. (2004). *Learning reconsidered*. Washington, DC: Author.

Astin, A. W. (1977). *Four critical years: Effects of college on beliefs, attitudes, and knowledge*. San Francisco: Jossey-Bass.

Astin, A. W. (1984). Student involvement: A developmental theory for higher education. *Journal of College Student Personnel*, 25, 297-308.

Astin, A. W. (1985). *Achieving educational excellence: A critical assessment of priorities and practices in higher education*. San Francisco: Jossey-Bass.

Baxter Magolda, M. B. (2001). *Making their own way*. Sterling, VA: Stylus.

Baxter Magolda, M. B. (2003). Identity and learning: Student affairs' role in transforming higher education. *Journal of College Student Development*, 44(2) 231-246.

Belenky, M. F., Clinchy, B. M., Goldberger, N. R., & Tarule, J. M. (1986). *Women's ways of knowing: The development of self, voice, and mind*. New York: Basic Books.

Brown, R. D. (1978). How evaluation can make a difference. In G. R. Hanson (Ed.), *Evaluating program effectiveness*. San Francisco: Jossey-Bass.

Brown, R. D., & DeCoster, D. A. (1982). *Mentoring-transcript systems for promoting student growth*. San Francisco: Jossey-Bass.

Dewey, J. (1916). *Democracy and education*. New York: The MacMillan Company.

Erwin, T. D. (1991). *Assessing student learning and development*. San Francisco: Jossey-Bass.

Heath, D. H. (1968). *Growing up in college: Liberal education and maturity*. San Francisco: Jossey-Bass.

Lewin, K. (1936). *Principles of typological psychology*. New York: McGraw-Hill.

Loevinger, J., & Wessler, R. (1970). *Measuring ego development: Construction and use of a sentence completion test*. San Francisco: Jossey-Bass.

Passon, A. H. (1987). Reporting the results of evaluation studies. *International Journal of Educational Research*, 2, 115-123.

Perry, W. G., Jr. (1968). *Forms of intellectual and ethical development in the college years: A scheme*. New York: Holt, Rinehart & Winston.

Piaget, J. (1952). *The origins of intelligence in children*. New York: International Universities Press.

Sanford, N. (1967). *Where colleges fail*. San Francisco: Jossey-Bass.

Strange, C.C., & Banning, J. H. (2001). *Education by design*, San Francisco: Jossey-Bass.

Wergin, J. F. (1989). Politics and assessment in the university. In T. W. Banta (Ed.), *Assessment update: Progress, trends, and practices in higher education*. San Francisco: Jossey-Bass.